THE WORLD O

Science
SATs Revision

John Sadler and Emily Clare

Contents

Page

4–5	A character reference	Chromosomes
6–7	Looking good	Inheritance
8–9	Successful breeding	Selective breeding
10–11	Fit for life	Healthy living
12–13	Warning!	Dangers of smoking
14–15	Looking after your body	Unhealthy living
16–17	We need light to grow	Photosynthesis and respiration
18–19	Nature's food factories	Functions of a leaf
20–21	Brainstorm	Chromosomes
22–23	Test your knowledge 1	
24–25	You are what you eat	Food for humans
26–27	Green fingers	Fertilisers
28–29	Pesticide problem	Pesticides
30–31	K Ni Fe and S P I N metals – and non-metals	Metals and non-metals
32–33	Worth their salt	Salts
34–35	A balancing act	Chemical equations
36–37	Are we tarnished for life?	Reactivity series 1
38–39	The power game	Reactivity series 2
40–41	Brainstorm	Metals and non-metals
42–43	Test your knowledge 2	
44–45	Acid rain	Pollution

46–47	Are we getting dirtier?	The greenhouse effect and the ozone layer
48–49	Fuels	Different types of fuels
50–51	Energising facts	Simple cells
52–53	Here to stay	Conservation of mass
54–55	Energy for life	Energy changes
56–57	Passing through	Series and parallel circuits
58–9	Warming up	Energy transfer
60–61	Brainstorm	Energy
62–63	Test your knowledge 3	
64–65	The big attraction	Gravity
66–67	Keep on moving	Solar system
68–69	Moving fast	Speed, distance and time
70–71	Quick, quick, slow	Effect of forces
72–73	3, 2, 1 jump!	Air resistance
74–75	The pressure is on	Pressure, force and area
76–77	Move it!	Levers
78–79	Just a moment	Moments
80–81	Brainstorm	Force
82–83	Test your knowledge 4	
84–89	Practice paper	
90–91	Glossary	
92–96	Answers	

A character reference

The human genome

The genome in humans is distributed among 23 pairs of chromosomes. Each chromosome carries genes along its length. A gene is made of deoxyribonucleic acid – <u>DNA</u>. As you can see in the diagram DNA is a very long, spiral-shaped molecule with a ladder-like structure. The rungs of the ladder are made of <u>bases</u>. There are four different bases called G, A, T and C. The sequence of these bases is called the <u>genetic</u> <u>code</u>. The code instructs cells to make proteins. Human DNA is more than three billion bases in length, and so a vast array of different proteins can be made.

Gene therapy

A person with a genetic disorder has a fault in their genetic code. A change or mutation in the base sequence of one <u>gene</u> causes single-gene disorders, e.g. cystic fibrosis and sickle-cell anaemia. There are more than 6000 known single-gene disorders and they occur in about one out of every 200 births.

Now that geneticists (scientists who study genes) have the HGP map for humans, it is hoped that they will be able to replace the faulty gene with a healthy one, a process called <u>gene</u> <u>therapy</u>, and so cure genetic disorders. However, this is still some way off in the future.

Ethics and morals

There is a fine line to tread between being able to treat genetic disorders in the future and using the HGP information responsibly. There is much discussion amongst scientists and governing bodies as to how to use the information for the good of human beings. For example, in the future you may be able to find out what illnesses you are likely to develop later in your life, and how long you are likely to live for.

Meiosis

- Each of your parents has 46 <u>chromosomes</u>. When you were conceived a sperm from your father and an egg from your mother fused to produce a single cell called a <u>zygote</u>. Sperm and eggs are special sex cells called <u>gametes</u>.

- Gametes have 23 chromosomes; half the number of chromosomes (and hence half the number of genes) of all other human cells. The process by which the chromosome number is halved is called <u>meiosis</u>.

- Meiosis occurs when the gametes (sperm and ova) are being made. A human zygote contains the full number of chromosomes (46), and the full number of genes; half from the father and half from the mother.

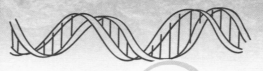

The diagram shows meiosis (produces gametes) and <u>fertilisation</u>. For simplicity only six of the 46 chromosomes in the parent cell are shown. The chromosomes are coloured to help you.

You have an equal number of chromosomes from each of your parents and this is why you have similar characteristics to them.

EXAMINER'S TOP TIPS

If a question asks you to draw the arrangement of chromosomes during meiosis and mitosis, remember to draw only one or two so that the process is simpler for you to show (and will save you time).

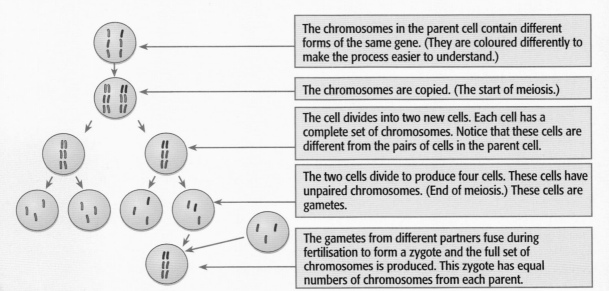

The chromosomes in the parent cell contain different forms of the same gene. (They are coloured differently to make the process easier to understand.)

The chromosomes are copied. (The start of meiosis.)

The cell divides into two new cells. Each cell has a complete set of chromosomes. Notice that these cells are different from the pairs of cells in the parent cell.

The two cells divide to produce four cells. These cells have unpaired chromosomes. (End of meiosis.) These cells are gametes.

The gametes from different partners fuse during fertilisation to form a zygote and the full set of chromosomes is produced. This zygote has equal numbers of chromosomes from each parent.

Meiosis (shown with only six chromosomes)

Mitosis

<u>Mitosis</u> is the process in which a cell nucleus divides into two identical nuclei and the number of chromosomes stays the same. The diagram shows mitosis taking place in a cell containing four of the 46 chromosomes. The new cells that are formed are used for growth or repair. You produce about 25 million new cells every second!

Two pairs of chromosomes.

The chromosomes double.

The chromosomes separate into two groups.

The nucleus divides into two new nuclei, each with four chromosomes. The rest of the cell divides to form two new, identical cells.

Mitosis (shown with only four chromosomes)

KEY FACTS

⬆ **Each chromosome carries thousands of genes.**

➡ **Each gene contains the instruction for a single feature of an organism.**

⬇ **All human cells have 46 chromosomes, except for the gametes (sperm and ova) which have 23 chromosomes.**

⬆ **A zygote (cell formed by fusion of sperm and ova during fertilisation) has 46 chromosomes.**

Looking good

Dear Santer,
Please may I have a baby brother with brown eyes and hair like me? I'm very ill. I think that the only way I will be able to grow old is to have a baby EXACTLY like me to help me by giving me special cells to make me better. How are you and how are your raindeers? It is amazing how you can get all around the Wirld in one night.
luv
Charles aged 6

A baby boy or girl?

A young boy suffering from faulty genes could have written this letter. Charles' disease was not passed on to him from his parents. A <u>mutation</u> (fault) has occurred in one of his genes and it is this that has given him the illness. A sibling will have similar DNA and it might be possible to replace the faulty gene with a healthy copy.

At present it is illegal in the UK for parents to select an embryo that will have a tissue match for their seriously ill child to cure him or her. However, it is lawful to select the sex of a child if there is a history of an inherited disease that is passed on by the male only or the female only. Genetic diseases such as haemophilia and muscular dystrophy occur only in male babies. Doctors can sort sperm and select only those sperm that will produce girls so that parents can avoid passing on these diseases to their children.

Sex determination

The sex of humans and other mammals is determined by <u>X chromosomes</u> and <u>Y chromosomes</u>. These are called the <u>sex chromosomes</u> and can be distinguished from other chromosomes because the Y chromosome is shorter than the X chromosome with which it is paired, forming an 'odd' pair. A male has an 'X and Y' pair, and a female has an 'X and X' pair.

If a female egg is fertilised by a sperm carrying a 'Y' chromosome the baby will be a boy; if a female egg is fertilised by a sperm carrying an 'X' chromosome the baby will be a girl. The father's sperm determines the sex of the baby. You can see from the diagram that the chance of Charles getting the baby brother he wants is 50:50.

	Male 'XY'	
gametes	**X**	**Y**
Female 'XX' **X**	XX	XY
X	XX	XY
Offspring:	50% female	50% male

Traits

People have different features, e.g. skin colour, hair colour, nose shape etc. All these characteristics, called <u>traits</u>, help to make each one of us unique. We inherited these traits from our parents.

Siblings are not identical in their looks, but they share certain traits. People will usually be able to tell that they are from the same family.

Genotypes and phenotypes

A gene can exist in two or more forms but only one of these forms is present in a chromosome. The forms are called alleles. Each <u>allele</u> is paired because the chromosomes are arranged in pairs. One allele in the pair may be dominant, recessive or equal to the other.

<u>Dominant</u> alleles show their effect whether there are one or two of them in the pair, and are written as a capital letter, e.g. B for brown eye colour. <u>Recessive</u> alleles show their effect only if both genes are in the pair, and are written as lower case letters, e.g. b for blue eye colour.

The trait that an organism shows is called its <u>phenotype</u>. The gene combination that determines the phenotype is called the <u>genotype</u>.

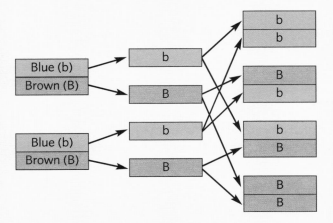

- We can use BB, Bb and bb as shorthand ways of describing genotypes for eye colour as shown in the diagram.

- Assume Charles' parents both have the genotypes shown and that the dominant allele is brown, B, and the recessive allele is blue, b.

- A parent passes on only one of its paired genes to its child. Since brown is the dominant colour, the chances of Charles' sibling having brown eyes is three in four chance or 3 : 1 ratio – 3 brown : 1 blue.

Twins

Twins are two babies that develop at the same time in the uterus and who are born within minutes of each other.

<u>Identical</u> <u>twins</u> develop from a single zygote. The zygote halves between days one and 14 of conception and forms two cells capable of developing into two identical individuals. Identical twins have identical DNA; they have the same genotype but different phenotypes. For example, their fingerprints are different.

<u>Non-identical</u> <u>twins</u> are formed when two eggs are released from the ovary in the same month and both are fertilised. The genetic make-up of non-identical twins is similar to that of siblings.

Research on identical twins has shown that the environment can alter their phenotype. For example, identical twins brought up under different conditions might have different heights and weights but their genotypes will remain identical.

phenotype = genotype + environment

KEY FACTS

⬆ **Dominant alleles always show their effect.**

➡ **The term genotype describes an organism in terms of its combination of genes.**

⬇ **The term phenotype is a description of an organism based on its observable characteristics.**

Successful breeding

And the winner is ...

Two different breeds of dog that have been exhibited at Crufts Dog Show are shown in the photographs. At Crufts the finest examples of many dog breeds are represented. These dogs are the results of years of careful breeding programmes undertaken by members of each Breed Society. Originally, dogs

were bred for a purpose, e.g. hunting or pulling sleds across snow, but now more and more breeds are continued just for the pleasure of their looks. The two dogs in the photographs have different ears, tails, legs and colouring; but they, and all other dogs, have the same number of chromosomes.

Chromosome numbers in different species

Each species has a definite number of chromosomes. Chromosome numbers for various species are listed below. The number of chromosomes a species has does not depend on the size or the complexity of the organism. The chromosome number is always even because chromosomes are arranged in pairs.

Organism	No. of chromosomes	Organism	No. of chromosomes	Organism	No. of chromosomes
ant	2	frog	36	human	46
cat	38	fly	8	mouse	40
chicken	78	goldfish	94	onion	16
dog	78	horse	64	potato	48

Selective breeding

Selective breeding is the process in which animals and plants that show desirable traits are selected and bred from. In this way hopefully a proportion of the offspring shows all the traits selected for.

The example shown is based on the work of Gregor Mendel, who studied pea plants and cross-bred them to produce offspring showing combinations of the desired traits.

Select plants that show desired traits

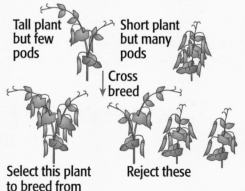

Tall plant but few pods

Short plant but many pods

Cross breed

Select this plant to breed from

Reject these

Economic benefits of selective breeding

- Selective breeding in animals: this has produced all the different breeds of dogs from original wild dogs.

- Selective breeding in plants. Farmers are able to produce large apples that have no scab (a fungal disease); pink potatoes that are resistant to blight; or cereal crops that are resistant to leaf disease.

- Selective breeding in farm animals. Farmers are able to produce cows that produce more milk, and hens that lay more eggs. It is now possible to breed hens that lay 240 eggs a year – the average in the 1940s was about 120 eggs per year.

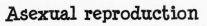

Asexual reproduction

- <u>Asexual</u> <u>reproduction</u> does not involve the union of sex cells (gametes) to produce a zygote and only one parent is involved. The offspring is identical to the parent.
- Examples of organisms that reproduce by asexual reproduction are bacteria and amoeba. They both reproduce by the process of mitosis; the cells split into two identical cells. A new, genetically identical individual is produced.
- Asexual reproduction does not allow genetic variation, but guarantees reproduction (no dependence on others).
- Asexual reproduction rapidly increases the numbers of an organism, and keeps its desired combination of traits.

Examples of plants that use different methods of asexual reproduction are shown in the table.

Plant	Method of asexual reproduction
garlic	bulbs
bindweed	rhizomes
potato	tubers
strawberry	runners

Cloning

The process of making identical organisms by asexual reproduction is called <u>cloning</u>. <u>Grafting</u> and <u>budding</u> are methods used to clone plants. The diagram shows grafting.

When you hear the word 'cloning' you may think of 'Dolly the Sheep' who was the first animal ever to be cloned and to survive any length of time. Dolly was born on 24 February 1997. On 23 April, 1998 Dolly gave birth to a female lamb named 'Bonnie'. So Dolly was not just a successful clone when she was born; she succeeded in growing and maturing to the adult reproductive stage. Since these events there has been much discussion about the possibility of cloning humans. But cloning could bring many risks, including:

- abuse of technology
- emotional upset
- serious damage to health.

Clean cuts made

Graft from the new plant is bound to a growing second plant

KEY FACTS

⬆ **Selective breeding is the method of choosing individuals with particular desired inherited traits to cross-breed (mate).**

➡ **New breeds of animals and plants have been produced by selective breeding.**

⬇ **In cloning (asexual reproduction) all the genetic material comes from one parent.**

Fit for life

Try the following fitness test.

Circle **Y** for 'yes', or **N** for 'no' after each of the questions.

See if you are as fit as you think!

After running for five minutes:

1 Are you warmer than usual and slightly sweaty, but not dripping?   Y   N
2 Can you carry on a conversation while running?   Y   N
3 Could you comfortably continue running for another five minutes at the same speed without stopping?   Y   N
4 Is your breathing deeper and more rapid than usual but not uncontrolled?   Y   N
5 Is your heart beating faster than usual but not racing?   Y   N

Scores:

If you have answered 'yes' to:

➤ four or more questions, you are fit, but keep on taking regular exercise
➤ two or three questions, you need to take more exercise
➤ none or one question, you definitely need to take more exercise.

Each day you should try to do one of the following:

✓ walk quickly for 30 minutes
✓ bicycle briskly for 20 minutes
✓ swim for 20 minutes.

You could also help in the garden or polish the car. Any form of activity will help you stay fit!

Why exercise?

Taking regular exercise is good for you. Regular exercise:

• helps you to maintain a healthy weight
• increases your strength and endurance
• makes your lungs and heart stronger (your heart has to beat over 100 000 times a day).

However, too much exercise can be dangerous, especially for girls, who may develop amenorrhoea (cessation of monthly periods).

Fitness depends on the individual and the type of career they have, e.g. an office worker tends not to be as physically fit as a manual worker. A person can control their fitness level by making lifestyle choices, e.g. regular exercise at the swimming pool or running for 15 minutes at the start of their day several times a week.

From food to muscle

Your body is like a car. A car needs fuel, air and water; it needs to be kept well oiled and all the different parts have to interact smoothly. Fuel burns in air to give the car energy.

Your body's fuel is food. You need an efficient digestive system to break down the large molecules present in the food you eat into smaller molecules. You also need water and oxygen (in the air breathed in through your lungs) for <u>respiration</u> to occur. Respiration is a reaction between sugar (carbohydrate) and oxygen that produces carbon dioxide, water and energy.

carbohydrate + oxygen $\rightarrow$ carbon dioxide + water + energy

Strong, healthy lungs are important so that you can breathe in enough air to help the respiration process. A healthy heart is also essential as it is the pump that pushes the blood around your body. The blood carries food and oxygen to every living cell in your body. It is inside the cells that respiration takes place.

Breathing

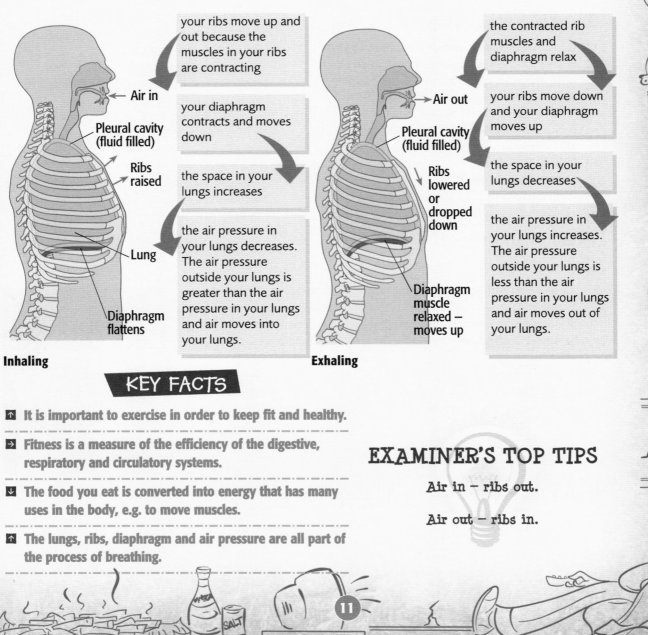

your ribs move up and out because the muscles in your ribs are contracting

Air in

Pleural cavity (fluid filled)

Ribs raised

your diaphragm contracts and moves down

the space in your lungs increases

the air pressure in your lungs decreases. The air pressure outside your lungs is greater than the air pressure in your lungs and air moves into your lungs.

Lung

Diaphragm flattens

Inhaling

the contracted rib muscles and diaphragm relax

Air out

Pleural cavity (fluid filled)

Ribs lowered or dropped down

your ribs move down and your diaphragm moves up

the space in your lungs decreases

the air pressure in your lungs increases. The air pressure outside your lungs is less than the air pressure in your lungs and air moves out of your lungs.

Diaphragm muscle relaxed – moves up

Exhaling

KEY FACTS

⬆ It is important to exercise in order to keep fit and healthy.

➡ Fitness is a measure of the efficiency of the digestive, respiratory and circulatory systems.

⬇ The food you eat is converted into energy that has many uses in the body, e.g. to move muscles.

⬆ The lungs, ribs, diaphragm and air pressure are all part of the process of breathing.

EXAMINER'S TOP TIPS

Air in – ribs out.

Air out – ribs in.

Warning!

SMOKING KILLS

SMOKING IS ADDICTIVE

SMOKING WHEN PREGNANT HARMS YOUR BABY

YOUR SMOKING CAN HARM OTHERS

Cigarettes contain more than 4000 chemicals, most of which are harmful to our bodies. Cigarette manufacturers have to put government health warnings like those shown above on cigarette packets.

Smoking statistics

- Non-smokers outlive smokers by about 15 years.
- Smoking causes 20% of all deaths from cancer, heart disease and strokes (nine out of ten lung cancer deaths are the result of smoking).
- In one week, about 1600 people in the UK die from smoking-related illnesses (62% men and 38% women).
- One-third of all men and women under the age of 44 in the UK smoke.
- A person who smokes 20 cigarettes a day is twice as likely to have a heart attack as a non-smoker.
- The highest proportion of smoking-related deaths is in Liverpool, Knowsley (on Merseyside) and Tower Hamlets in east London.
- Smoking kills more people in the UK than HIV/AIDS, car accidents, murder, suicide and illegal drug use combined.
- In a year, smoking causes the deaths of over three million people in the World (about six people a minute).
- If the current trend in smoking patterns continues, about 500 million people who are alive today will die as a result of smoking.

What is in smoke?

When people smoke they inhale carbon monoxide, nicotine and tar.

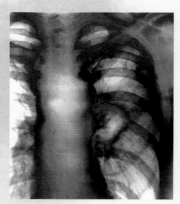

- Carbon monoxide is formed by the incomplete combustion of tobacco in air (oxygen). It diffuses into the blood and occupies the place in the red blood cells that normally carries oxygen and thus prevents oxygen from being carried efficiently around the body. Carbon monoxide in the blood also increases the chance of cardiovascular disease (damage to the heart).
- Nicotine is highly <u>addictive</u>. Nicotine stimulates the central nervous system. Stimulation is followed by depression and fatigue, leading the addict to seek more nicotine to get another 'up'. The only way to give up smoking is if the person really, really wants to. Nicotine also causes a short-term increase in blood pressure, heart rate and flow of blood from the heart. It causes the arteries to narrow and harden (become less stretchy and elastic), so the person is more likely to suffer from cardiovascular disease.
- Tar in smoke coats the surface of the <u>alveoli</u> in the lungs decreasing the efficiency of gas exchange. Tar causes cancer of the lung tissue. The photograph shows a lung from a smoker who died of lung cancer. The white area at the top of the lung is the cancer and the blackened areas covering the rest of the lung are tar deposits.

Effects of smoking

As well as lung cancer and cardiovascular disease, smoking increases the risk of suffering from the following.

- Emphysema. Smoking destroys the elasticity of the lungs by damaging the tissue that pulls the lungs back together after using muscles that allow us to inhale air. So, when it's time to breathe again it is much more difficult. To find out how it feels to have emphysema take a deep breath and hold it. Now without letting out any air, take another deep breath and hold that one. Now take one more breath. The second or third breath is what it feels like to breathe when you have emphysema. Emphysema is a disease where it is extremely difficult to exhale air.
- Bronchitis. This is inflammation of the tubes in the lungs (bronchi) and can be caused by smoke inhalation. The tiny hairs (cilia) that move mucus up and down to clean the tubes are damaged by smoke and stop working. The air passages become clogged and more mucus is formed. This collects in the tubes and causes the characteristic cough of bronchitis ('smoker's cough') as the lungs try to clear the mucus.
- Low birth-weight babies. Women who smoke during pregnancy are more likely to give birth to smaller babies. Smoking can affect the brain development and general health of the baby, as well as increasing the chance of it being stillborn (dead).

Passive smoking

Passive smoking is breathing in the smoke made by smokers. Some of the short-term effects are:

- eye irritation
- headache
- sickness
- asthma attacks.

Long-term effects of passive smoking are:

- lung cancer
- cardiovascular disease.

Passive smoking has also been linked to sudden infant death (cot death) by some scientists. In England over 17 000 children under the age of five are admitted to hospital because of illness caused by passive smoking.

KEY FACTS

- ↑ Cigarettes contain carbon monoxide, nicotine and tar.
- → Smoking is the cause of many diseases, e.g. lung cancer, cardiovascular disease, bronchitis and emphysema.
- ↓ Nicotine is addictive and makes it hard to give up smoking.
- ↑ Nicotine hardens the arteries, forcing the heart to beat faster.

EXAMINER'S TOP TIPS

It is carbon monoxide that is poisonous, NOT carbon dioxide. (Carbon dioxide is essential for breathing.)

Looking after your body

I thought I was all right

Have none for the road

Come on Dave, just one more

Don't take your car for a drink

Don't drink and drive

I've only had a couple

I'm dying for a drink

It takes less than you think for your driving to be impaired

Despite the efforts of the Royal Society for the Prevention of Accidents (RoSPA) and other organisations, some people choose to drink and drive. In a survey carried out by the road safety charity 'Brake' in 2004, 3% of all drivers admitted that they drove whilst being over the limit at least three or more times in a year. Their reasons for doing this included that they 'felt safe to drive'; and that 'there was no alternative means of transport'. In 2003, 560 people were killed in drink-drive related crashes; a further 2600 were seriously injured and 19 000 were slightly injured.

Chemical body damage

Alcohol is a <u>drug</u>. A drug is a chemical substance that changes the way the body and/or mind works.

- Alcohol slows down reaction times so making driving a car whilst under the influence of alcohol very dangerous to the driver and other road and footpath users.
- Alcohol reduces inhibitions and can lead people to behave irresponsibly.

Harmful effects of alcohol

Alcohol is sometimes called a 'social drug'. It is a legal drug but is only safe if consumed in controlled amounts. Once alcohol is swallowed it is rapidly absorbed into the bloodstream from the stomach. The first reactions take place in the brain. It is estimated that 15 million working days are lost each year in the UK due to alcoholism.

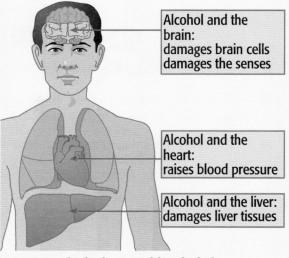

Alcohol and the brain: damages brain cells damages the senses

Alcohol and the heart: raises blood pressure

Alcohol and the liver: damages liver tissues

Damage to the body caused by alcohol

Physical body damage

The body can be damaged by physical processes as well as by chemicals.

Exercise is of benefit to health when done in moderation; however extreme and sustained levels of exercise can cause physical damage to the body, for example the <u>joints</u>. Gradual wear and tear of joints through normal use occurs with age, but this process can be speeded up if extreme forces are applied through over-vigorous exercise or injury. Worn-out joints are very painful and this may mean an operation is necessary to replace the affected joint with an artificial one.

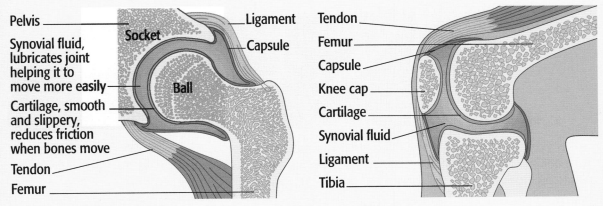

Hip, a ball and socket joint

Pelvis
Synovial fluid, lubricates joint helping it to move more easily
Cartilage, smooth and slippery, reduces friction when bones move
Tendon
Femur
Socket
Ball
Ligament
Capsule

Knee, a hinge joint

Tendon
Femur
Capsule
Knee cap
Cartilage
Synovial fluid
Ligament
Tibia

Two of the most common joints in the body to be affected are the hips and the knees. The diagrams show the structure of these two joints.

- The <u>ball</u> <u>and</u> <u>socket</u> joint in the hip and shoulder gives movement in all directions, i.e. circular movement.
- The <u>hinge</u> <u>joint</u> in the knee and elbow gives movement forwards and backwards in only one plane.

During an operation to replace a damaged hip joint, affected bone tissue and cartilage are removed from the joint. The healthy parts of the hip are left . The head of the femur (the ball) and the socket are replaced with artificial parts made from a material that allows a friction-free, gliding motion.

Sports men and women often damage the cartilage in their knee joints. The blood supply to cartilage is very small so these types of injury can take a long time to heal. The operation to replace a damaged knee joint is similar to that of the hip joint replacement.

KEY FACTS

↱ **Drinking alcohol reduces a person's reaction time and reduces their inhibitions.**

↳ **Legal drugs can be very dangerous unless taken under supervised conditions.**

↓ **There are two main types of joints: ball and socket joint and hinge joint.**

EXAMINER'S TOP TIPS

Make sure you give the correct uses. Muscles can only pull and relax. (They do not push.)

We need light to grow

Q Which living organism can make its food? Is it A, B, C or D?

A   C

B   D

A C, the plant.

Green plants are the only living things that can make their own food. Babies rely on their parents; fish eat algae and other smaller fish and earthworms eat bacteria and fungi. Eating food made from plants provides you with the energy you need to function.

Photosynthesis

Plants get their energy by a process called <u>photosynthesis</u>. Photosynthesis takes place in the green leaves.

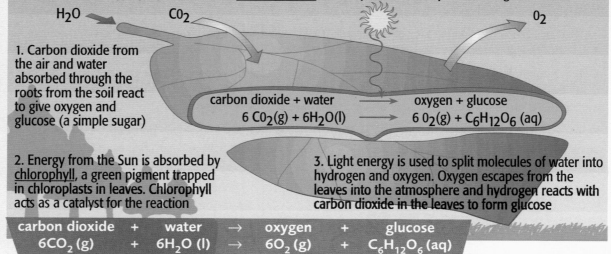

H_2O CO_2 O_2

1. Carbon dioxide from the air and water absorbed through the roots from the soil react to give oxygen and glucose (a simple sugar)

carbon dioxide + water   oxygen + glucose

$6 CO_2(g) + 6H_2O(l)$ $6 O_2(g) + C_6H_{12}O_6 (aq)$

2. Energy from the Sun is absorbed by <u>chlorophyll</u>, a green pigment trapped in chloroplasts in leaves. Chlorophyll acts as a catalyst for the reaction

3. Light energy is used to split molecules of water into hydrogen and oxygen. Oxygen escapes from the leaves into the atmosphere and hydrogen reacts with carbon dioxide in the leaves to form glucose

carbon dioxide	+	water	→	oxygen	+	glucose
$6CO_2$ (g)	+	$6H_2O$ (l)	→	$6O_2$ (g)	+	$C_6H_{12}O_6$ (aq)

During photosynthesis, light energy from the Sun is changed into chemical energy. The chemical energy is stored as sugar (mainly glucose) in the plant's leaves. Glucose molecules join together (<u>polymerise</u>) to form large starch molecules stored in the leaves. Starch is only slightly soluble in water and can readily be converted back into sugars. It is the <u>chemical</u> <u>energy</u> in starch that all <u>consumers</u> use.

Biomass

<u>Biomass</u> is the term used to describe all the organic matter produced by photosynthesis that exists on Earth. The energy in biomass is obtained from the Sun. Energy can be extracted from biomass. One way is to burn it. Another method, used in Brazil, is to extract the sugar in sugar cane. The sugar is dissolved in water and fermented to make alcohol that is used instead of petrol as a fuel for engines.

Respiration

Plants need to use stored chemical energy in order to grow, transport nutrients, reproduce and protect themselves. They use oxygen from the air and sugars stored to make carbon dioxide and water. This process is called respiration and it releases energy.

$$\text{glucose} + \text{oxygen} \rightarrow \text{carbon dioxide} + \text{water} + \text{energy}$$
$$C_6H_{12}O_6 \text{ (aq)} + 6O_2 \text{ (g)} \rightarrow 6CO_2 \text{ (g)} + 6H_2O \text{ (l)}$$

Respiration is the opposite of photosynthesis. Photosynthesis can only take place during daylight whereas respiration takes place all the time.

Comparing photosynthesis and respiration

Photosynthesis	Respiration
Uses water	Gives off water
Uses carbon dioxide	Gives off carbon dioxide
Gives off oxygen	Uses oxygen
Makes sugars (glucose) and starch	Breaks down glucose and starch
Requires light	Occurs all the time
Takes in energy	Gives out energy
Occurs only in cells with chlorophyll	Occurs in cells of most living organisms
$6CO_2(g) + 6H_2O(l) \rightarrow C_6H_{12}O_6(aq) + 6O_2(g)$	$C_6H_{12}O_6(aq) + 6O_2(g) \rightarrow 6CO_2(g) + 6H_2O(l)$

Photosynthesis reduces the amount of carbon dioxide in the atmosphere. Carbon dioxide combined with water in a green leaf makes starch. The presence of starch in a plant indicates that photosynthesis is taking place.

Testing for starch

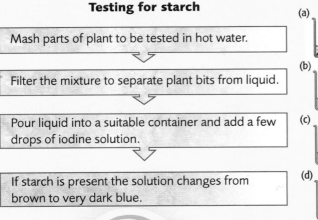

Mash parts of plant to be tested in hot water.

⬇

Filter the mixture to separate plant bits from liquid.

⬇

Pour liquid into a suitable container and add a few drops of iodine solution.

⬇

If starch is present the solution changes from brown to very dark blue.

(a)
(b)
(c)
(d)

KEY FACTS

↑ Carbon dioxide, water, chlorophyll and light are necessary for photosynthesis.

→ Respiration takes place all the time; photosynthesis occurs only in light.

↓ Biomass is the amount of living matter (or organisms) in a given volume or area.

↑ Iodine solution is used as a test for starch.

EXAMINER'S TOP TIPS

There are three reasons why vegetable root plants are bigger when they receive more light: more photosynthesis; more carbohydrate formed; more carbohydrate transported to the roots.

Nature's food factories

Q **All these herbivores have adapted so that they can gather their food efficiently. What is their main diet?**

Herbivores eat green leaves to provide them with energy to perform all their life functions. Competition for food from other herbivores is sometimes strong, especially in areas where droughts are frequent and severe making food scarce, so the animals have adapted by developing special features enabling them to graze different parts of trees and plants.

A **Green plants — nature's 'food factories'.**

Leaf structure and function

Just as herbivores have evolved to forage more efficiently, green plants have evolved the structure of their leaves to aid the process of photosynthesis. The following list and the illustration describe how the structure of a leaf promotes photosynthesis.

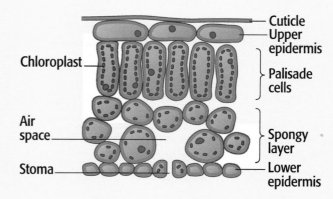

- Leaves provide a large surface area for maximum light absorption.
- The veins in a leaf give some support and provide channels for water and nutrients to flow through.
- The outer surface of the leaf has a waxy coating called the cuticle. The cuticle reduces evaporation of water from the leaf surface and protects the leaf from damage and disease.
- Below the cuticle are the epidermis cells. These maintain the shape of the leaf and produce the cuticle. They do not contain chloroplasts so they are relatively transparent, enabling light to pass through easily.
- The next layer of cells, the palisade cells, contain chloroplasts (chloroplasts contain a green pigment called chlorophyll). Palisade cells are thin and long providing a large surface area for light to enter. The chloroplasts contain chlorophyll and other pigments. It is here that photosynthesis takes place. Chloroplasts absorb light energy and convert it into chemical energy.
- The spongy layer contains loosely packed, rounded cells surrounded by spaces. Oxygen and carbon dioxide are stored in these spaces.
- Carbon dioxide enters the leaf through the stomata (small pores) and passes into the spongy layer. The stomata are mostly on the underside of the leaf. Stomata can open and close to either allow carbon dioxide from the air in or let oxygen formed during photosynthesis out.
- Leaves are very thin. Light and gases entering and leaving the leaf only have to travel short distances.

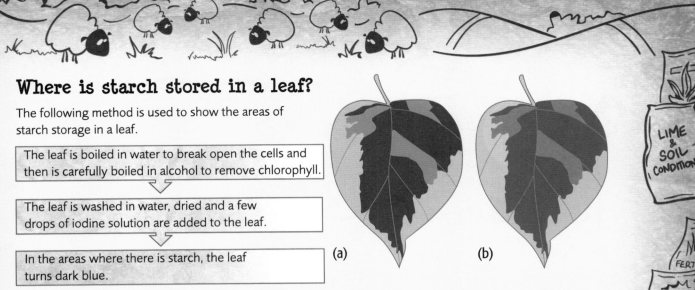

Where is starch stored in a leaf?

The following method is used to show the areas of starch storage in a leaf.

| The leaf is boiled in water to break open the cells and then is carefully boiled in alcohol to remove chlorophyll. |

⬇

| The leaf is washed in water, dried and a few drops of iodine solution are added to the leaf. |

⬇

| In the areas where there is starch, the leaf turns dark blue. |

(a)   (b)

When variegated plant leaves are tested for starch only the green areas of the leaf turn dark blue. This shows that starch is only found in the green part of the leaf, i.e. where there is chlorophyll. The illustration shows a variegated leaf before and after testing for starch.

Etiolation

A plant needs light to remain healthy. In the illustration the plant on the left has been grown under normal conditions and the plant on the right has received little light. It has long, weak stems, small leaves, and is a pale yellow colour. This plant has grown rapidly to increase its height to try to reach light. The pale colour is due to a lack of chlorophyll. This effect is called <u>etiolation</u>. If the plant was returned to the light it would turn green as photosynthesis resumed.

(a)   (b)

Production of oxygen

The experiment shows that during photosynthesis bubbles of gas are produced. A glowing splint re-ignites in the gas, showing that the gas is oxygen.

Explaining leaf-colour changes

Why do leaves change colour in autumn and bananas go yellow when they ripen? It is to do with light. As winter approaches the days get shorter so there is less light for photosynthesis and the leaves stop making chlorophyll.Most leaves contain small amounts of the pigments xanthophyll (yellow) and carotene (orange). Chlorophyll (green) masks these colours normally but they begin to show when there is less chlorophyll being made. When bananas ripen, they contain more xanthophyll and hardly any chlorophyll and turn yellow.

Oxygen

Water

Pondweed

KEY FACTS

⬆ **The palisade cells in a leaf contain chloroplasts – the site of photosynthesis.**

⬇ **Chlorophyll gives leaves their green colour.**

⬇ **Etiolation describes a plant that develops without chlorophyll because it has been kept in conditions where there is no sunlight.**

EXAMINER'S TOP TIPS

The parts of a leaf can be remembered by 'CUP CLASS': Cuticle; Upper epidermis; Palisade; Chloroplast; Lower epidermis; Air space; Spongy layer; Stoma.

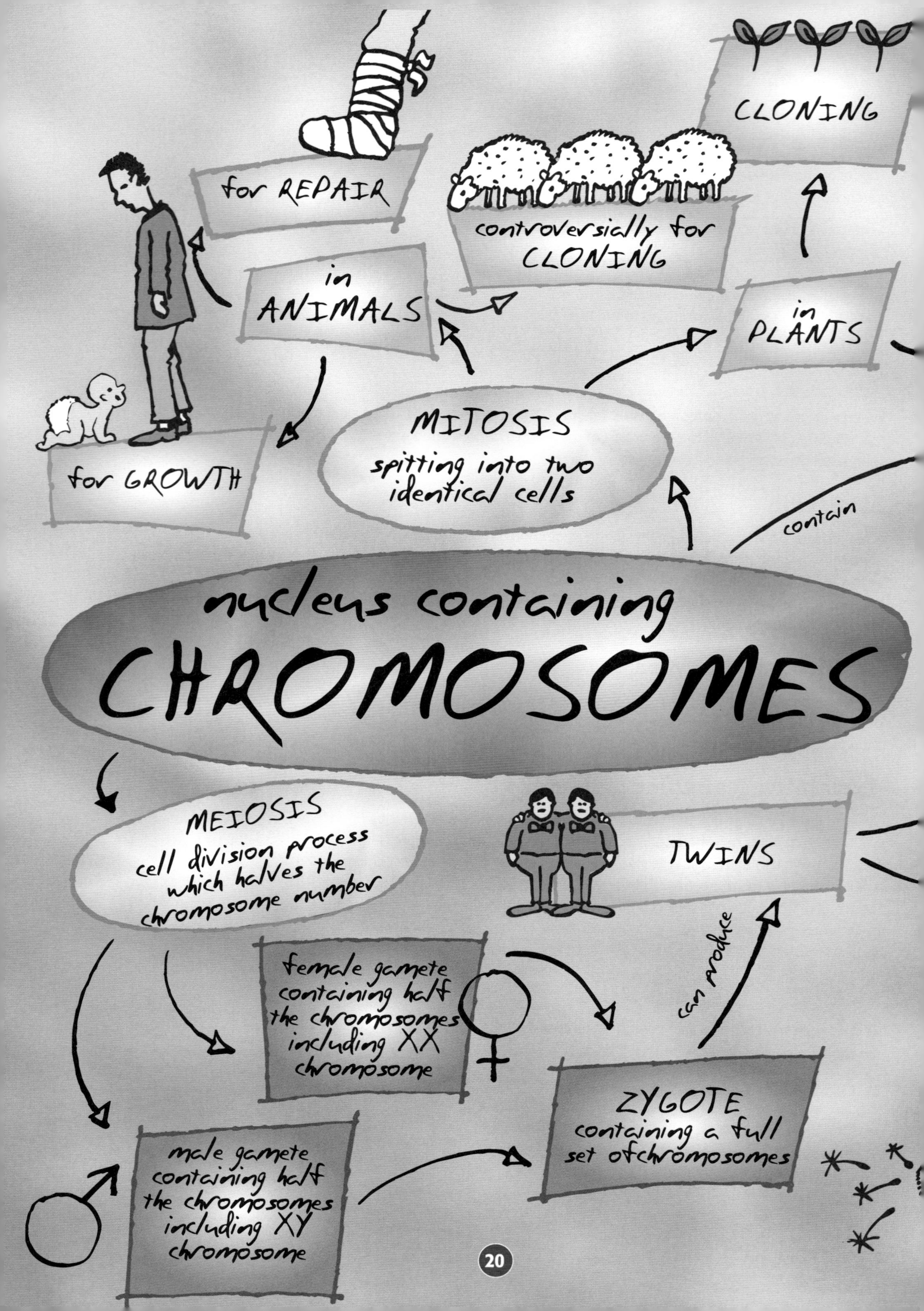

for REPAIR

controversially for
CLONING

CLONING

in
ANIMALS

in
PLANTS

for GROWTH

MITOSIS
spitting into two
identical cells

contain

nucleus containing
CHROMOSOMES

MEIOSIS
cell division process
which halves the
chromosome number

TWINS

female gamete
containing half
the chromosomes
including XX
chromosome

can produce

male gamete
containing half
the chromosomes
including XY
chromosome

ZYGOTE
containing a full
set of chromosomes

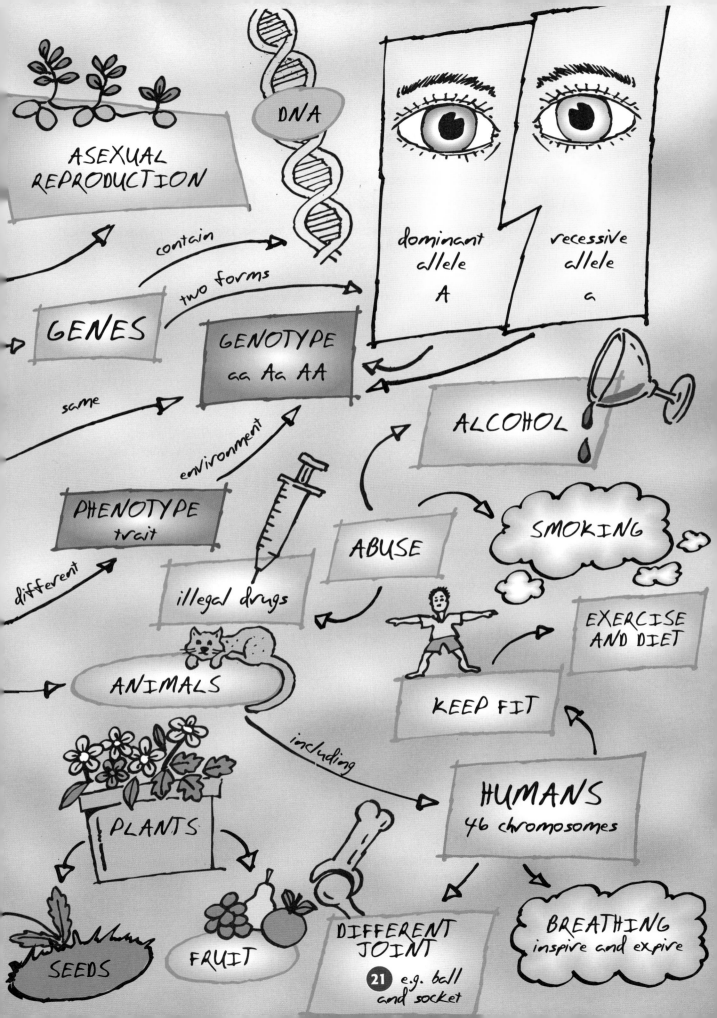

ASEXUAL REPRODUCTION

DNA

dominant allele A

recessive allele a

GENES

contain

two forms

GENOTYPE
aa Aa AA

same

ALCOHOL

environment

PHENOTYPE
trait

ABUSE

SMOKING

different

illegal drugs

EXERCISE AND DIET

ANIMALS

KEEP FIT

including

PLANTS

HUMANS
46 chromosomes

SEEDS

FRUIT

DIFFERENT JOINT
21 e.g. ball and socket

BREATHING
inspire and expire

Test your knowledge 1

1   A Shetland pony has 64 chromosomes.

a)   How many chromosomes will there be in a racehorse? Circle the correct answer.

A 32   **B** 64   **C** impossible to tell

b)   Egg cells and sperm cells are formed as a result of meiosis. How may chromosomes would there be in a Shetland pony sperm cell?

....

c)   Emily has a dominant gene for curly hair. The diagram below shows a family tree.

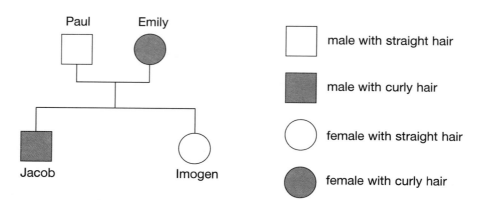

Use C for the dominant allele and c for the recessive allele.

(i)   What is Paul's genotype? Explain your answer.

....

(ii)   What is Emily's genotype? Explain your answer.

....

....

(iii)   If Paul and Emily have another child, there is a 50% chance that the child will be curly haired. Draw a genetic diagram to explain your answer.

(iv)   If Imogen married a man with dominant curly hair alleles (CC), what are the chances of them having a curly haired child? ....

(11 marks)

2 A cigarette was burned in oxygen in a fume cupboard using the apparatus below.

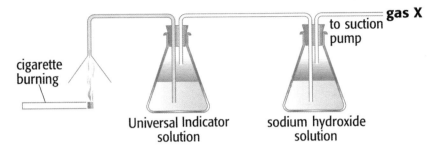

The products of burning are water vapour, carbon dioxide (acid gas), carbon monoxide (neutral gas), nicotine (neutral liquid), nitrogen dioxide (acid gas), sulphur dioxide (acid gas) and tar (acid liquid).

a) Explain how you know **gas X** contains only carbon monoxide.

....

....

b) Name four elements that MUST be present in cigarettes.

(i) .... (ii) ....

(iii) .... (iv) ....

c) Which substance causes addiction to smoking cigarettes? ....

(7 marks)

3 The pie chart shows the composition of inhaled air. By writing 'more', 'less' or 'same' in the column in the table below, show how exhaled air differs from inhaled air.

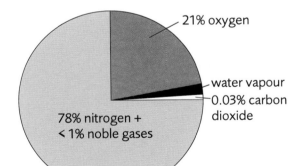

Percentage of substance in exhaled air	More/less/same
carbon dioxide	
nitrogen and noble gases	
oxygen	
water vapour	

(4 marks)

(Total 22 marks)

You are what you eat

It is estimated that every year the human race eats approximately 40% of the Earth's entire biomass.

Think about what you ate for your breakfast, mid-day and evening meals throughout last week. You probably had a variety of foods. But you and your family may eat one kind of food more often than others. For example, you may have cereal, bread and fruit juice for your breakfast every day. The food that makes up the bulk of a diet is called a <u>staple</u> <u>food</u>. It is estimated that 90% of homes have cereals in their homes and that 73% of us eat cereals for our breakfast.

Corn is the staple food for the population in Africa and rice is the staple food for the population in Asia. This is because both crops are easy to grow, and they are much cheaper than other foods. However, there are problems in relying on one type of food. If there is a drought many people will become malnourished. Cereals and rice supply only a small amount of the protein required for a balanced diet.

Our place in the food chain

[a]  [b]  [c]

- Plants are <u>producers</u> (make food by the process of photosynthesis). The energy for this reaction is obtained from the Sun.
- Sheep are herbivores (they eat only plants).
- Humans are <u>omnivores</u> (eat both plants and animals).
- Humans are consumers and <u>predators</u> at the top of the <u>food</u> <u>chain</u>. The energy we get from eating meat or vegetables has come from the Sun.

The food chain is very small and therefore not much energy is lost.

Where does our food come from?

Plants convert the glucose made by photosynthesis into starch which is stored in the roots, stems, leaves and seeds, so that they have a supply of food during the winter months. We benefit from this storage when we eat the food the plants have made. The table gives examples.

Plant	Starch stored in	Plant	Starch stored in
carrot	root	potato	root
pea	seed	apple	fruit
tomato	fruit	rice	seed
lettuce	leaves	mango	fruit

- Vegetables also contain other important substances, e.g. vitamin E is found in broccoli.
- Citrus fruits, e.g. oranges are a good source of vitamin C.

Plants also contain <u>incomplete</u> <u>proteins</u>. These are proteins that are missing one or two essential amino acids (building blocks of protein). Grains, nuts, beans and peas contain incomplete proteins. When you eat grain and beans together, your body helps them to combine to provide <u>complete</u> <u>proteins</u>. This is how vegetarians are able to have a healthy diet.

Balanced diet

A balanced diet provides your body with all the nutrients you need; it includes:

- carbohydrates
- fats and oils
- proteins
- vitamins
- fibre.

Your body also needs water and certain minerals, e.g. calcium for healthy bone growth and strong teeth.

EXAMINER'S TOP TIPS

If you are asked for uses of proteins, they are for growth, repair and maintenance.

KEY FACTS

- ◄ **Plants make starch by a process of photosynthesis.**
- ► **Starch made by photosynthesis is stored in various parts of the plant.**
- ↘ **Humans and other animals get their energy by eating plants.**

Green fingers

Darfur (home of the Fur people) is in Western Sudan. It is an area where sustaining life is extremely difficult. This is because there is an average annual rainfall of only 80 mm (compared with an annual rainfall of 1200 mm in the UK). To grow crops and maintain livestock herds the Fur people must have water. About 60% of the population suffers from the effects of drought.

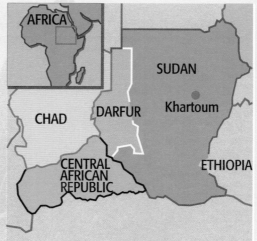

Water is the Fur's lifeblood. At present the use of what little water there is is inefficient (only 5% of rainwater is used for crop production and drinking) due mainly to poor water management systems. There are dam building and re-building projects underway. The rainwater from these dams will increase irrigation making more land suitable for cultivation. More vegetables, cash crops and plants can then be grown to feed the people and livestock. Sinking new wells will save women from having to travel long distances each day to fetch water.

Healthy plant growth

The main elements required by plants to produce good crops are shown in the table.

Element	Effect on plant
nitrogen (N)	promotes growth of leaves and stems
phosphorus (P)	promotes root system of root crops
potassium (K)	promotes flowering and fruiting
calcium, magnesium, sulphur	needed in small amounts; they are secondary nutrients
boron, copper, iron, manganese, molybdenum, zinc	needed in tiny amounts; they are trace elements

Farmers and gardeners have to look out for signs that their plants are missing specific nutrients.

- Lack of nitrogen: causes an excessive growth of roots. Cereal crops turn yellow.
- Lack of phosphorus and potassium: gives stunted root growth.

Fertilisers

When an area of ground is used to grow the same crop over and over again it is stripped of the nutrients (minerals) the plants need to thrive. These nutrients have to be replaced to achieve a good yield (amount of crop produced) by spreading fertilisers on the land. There are two main types of fertilisers – organic and inorganic.

- Organic fertilisers: occur naturally, e.g. garden compost and animal waste (contains a large proportion of straw). Organic fertilisers do not contain very high concentrations of nutrients and some nutrients might be missing. These fertilisers help to improve the soil and release their nutrients over a period of time. It does not really matter if you add too much organic fertiliser, e.g. manure.
- Inorganic fertilisers: are either extracted from the earth or they are manufactured. They contain all the nutrients needed by plants. Inorganic fertilisers are much more concentrated and need to be measured accurately to avoid damaging plants.

Disadvantages of fertilisers

- Excess fertiliser damages plant roots. Seedlings, young plants and plants that prefer acid soil are particularly vulnerable.
- Excess fertiliser can also damage the environment. Nitrates leach into streams, rivers and even get into tap water.
- A high level of nitrates in drinking water is harmful to babies.

Eutrophication

Fertilisers in water cause an increase in the growth of plants. This is called <u>eutrophication</u>. An increase in plant growth blocks out sunlight and underwater grasses die. These grasses provide food, shelter and breeding habitats for aquatic creatures. When the plants die and decompose, they further deplete the oxygen levels causing aquatic creatures to die.

Cost of fertilisation

The size of an average football pitch is 8000 m². The following shows how to calculate the cost of fertilising this pitch with 100 g per square metre all-purpose fertiliser at a price of 35p per kg sack.

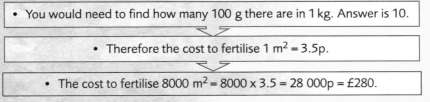

- You would need to find how many 100 g there are in 1 kg. Answer is 10.

- Therefore the cost to fertilise 1 m² = 3.5p.

- The cost to fertilise 8000 m² = 8000 x 3.5 = 28 000p = £280.

This is a lot of money, so it is important not to waste fertiliser. Another reason not to waste fertiliser is that both phosphorus and potassium are non-renewable resources.

KEY FACTS

◁ **Nitrogen, phosphorus and potassium are essential for plant growth together with small amounts of other elements.**

◱ **Fertilisers can be organic (occur naturally), or inorganic (man-made).**

◲ **Fertilisers contain nutrients in a concentrated form.**

◰ **Eutrophication is the build-up of fertilisers in water causing excess growth of plants.**

FERTILISER
N-P-K
5-7-9
N = Nitrogen
For strong green foliage
P = Phosphorus
For roots, fruit & flowers
K = Potassium (Potash)
Protects from disease & cold. Prevents water loss.

EXAMINER'S TOP TIPS

You may be asked what a plant needs to stay healthy.

K potassium	Know
P phosophorus	Plants'
N nitrogen	Nutrients

Pesticide problem

Pesticides debate

A pesticide is a chemical that kills harmful organisms and is used to control pests, e.g. insects, weeds or micro-organisms. Do you think farmers and gardeners should use pesticides?

Here are two sides of the debate.

YES to pesticides

'Rice is the basic food for 50% of the World's population. Asia consumes 90% of the World's rice. Without pesticides it is estimated that 83% of the harvest would be lost. Wheat is another basic food; over 33% of the World's population eat wheat in some form or other. Without pesticides over 36% of the wheat yield would be lost.'

'Some pesticides cause health problems. Small amounts remain in the food we eat. Excess pesticides can get washed into streams, rivers and seas. Here they may kill birds and fish. Some pesticides enter the food chain.'

NO to pesticides!

Harmful Effects of DDT are Confirmed

An insecticide called DDT is very good at killing insects. But birds who feed on the dead insects in large numbers are either dying or laying eggs that have very thin shells. When the birds incubate the eggs, the shells are breaking. The insecticide is also sprayed on water to kill insects such as mosquitoes.

plankton in water
0.00005 ppm DDT

→ small fish
0.04 ppm DDT

→ large fish
0.23 ppm DDT

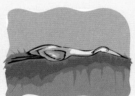
→ dead heron
3.57 ppm DDT

The illustration shows how animals at the top of the food chain are dying because DDT is concentrated as it travels up the food chain.

This newspaper article could have been written in the 1960s when DDT was used widely. The use of DDT in the UK is now banned and this has helped to reduce the number of birds being poisoned. However some birds, such as falcons, migrate to countries where DDT is permitted. To help protect these birds scientists take newly-laid eggs from nests and incubate them in laboratories.

Other methods of controlling plant pests

- Nematodes (type of worm): these kill slugs that feed on and damage vegetable crops. This is an example of biological control.
- Storage areas for grain: these could be made pest-proof.

Organically produced food

Some people only eat food that has been produced organically (without the use of man-made chemicals). <u>Organic</u> <u>food</u> is more expensive to buy as the natural methods used to control pests and diseases in the crops are more expensive.

Control of weeds

Plants, especially seedlings, need space in which to grow. Plants that are close together also have to compete for light, water and nutrients. One way to give plants more space is to get rid of weeds. <u>Herbicides</u> are used to kill weeds. They contain chemicals that are toxic to weeds and not the crop plants.

Optimum conditions for plant growth

The optimum (best) conditions for plant growth are:

- light and warmth
- carbon dioxide
- water
- nitrogen
- phosphorus
- potassium
- other elements in smaller amounts, e.g. selenium.

A greenhouse produces almost ideal conditions, but it does have some disadvantages as shown in the table.

Advantages of greenhouse environment	Disadvantages of greenhouse environment
Growing environment can be controlled, e.g. temperature, light and nutrients	Cost of keeping greenhouse warm can be expensive
Season of growing can be extended	Good greenhouses are not cheap
Protection from pests and weather	Unless kept clean, pests and diseases can build up
Increasing the amount of carbon dioxide in the atmosphere increases the rate of photosynthesis	Heat loss through air vents that let in air and carbon dioxide

Polytunnels are popular, especially for growing strawberries. They are cheaper than greenhouses and protect the plants from frost and wind, and so strawberries are produced earlier in the year compared with those grown outside.

KEY FACTS

- ◤ **Pesticides kill organisms. They are used to control pests, e.g. insects and weeds.**

- ◥ **Pesticides can have harmful effects on the environment, particularly if they get into the food chain.**

- ◢ **Greenhouses promote the growth of plants, but they must be kept clean and free of pests and diseases.**

EXAMINER'S TOP TIPS

Weeds stop vegetables from growing by shading the plants, by giving the vegetables less space to grow or by absorbing nutrients and/or water. Do not use vague answers, such as the vegetables had less space to grow or the 'weeds took the food'.

K Ni Fe and S P I N -
metals and non-metals

Q How many aluminium cans are thrown away on average each day in America?

Is it   50 million   100 million   200 million?

If these were laid end to end they would stretch for 13 600 miles. That is from Land's End to John O'Groats about 16 times!

A 200 million.

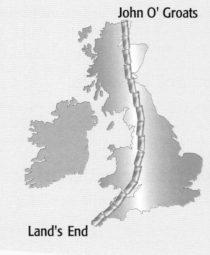

John O' Groats

Land's End

Physical properties of metals and non-metals

Physical properties are the characteristics of substances that can be measured, e.g. melting point and conduction of electricity. The table shows the physical properties of metals and non-metals.

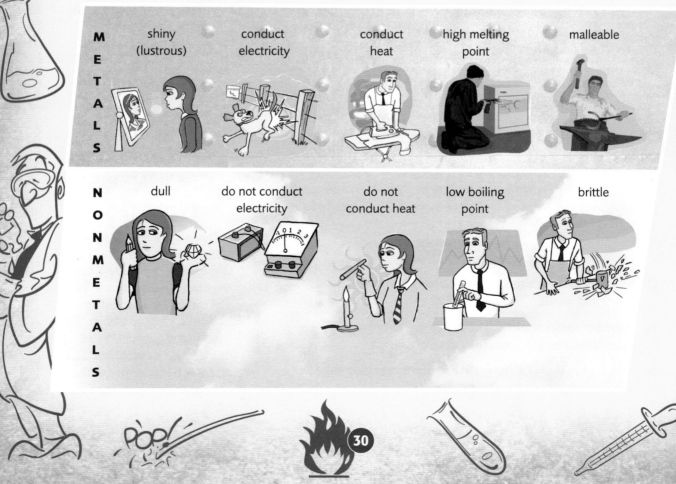

METALS

| shiny (lustrous) | conduct electricity | conduct heat | high melting point | malleable |

NONMETALS

| dull | do not conduct electricity | do not conduct heat | low boiling point | brittle |

Chemical properties of metals and non-metals

Chemical <u>properties</u> are properties that show how substances behave under different conditions, e.g. adding an acid.

Chemical properties of metals

Metals react with oxygen to form <u>basic</u> <u>oxides</u>. If the oxide dissolves in water it will form an <u>alkali</u>, e.g. magnesium oxide dissolves to form the alkali magnesium hydroxide:

magnesium (s)   +   oxygen (g) →   magnesium oxide (s)

magnesium oxide (s)   +   water (l)   →   magnesium hydroxide (aq)

Example

Metals react in oxygen

Metals react with acids to give hydrogen and a <u>salt</u>:

iron   +   sulphuric acid → hydrogen + iron sulphate

Metal and acid give salt and hydrogen

pop
metal
dilute acid

Chemical properties of non-metals

Non-metals react in oxygen.

Non-metals react with oxygen to form <u>acidic oxides</u>. If the oxide dissolves in water it will form an acid, e.g. sulphur trioxide and water form sulphuric acid:

sulphur (s)   +   oxygen (g) →   sulphur trioxide (g)

sulphur trioxide (g)   +   water (l)   →   sulphuric acid (aq)

Non-metal reacts in oxygen

They do not react with acids: Non-metals and acid; no reaction

carbon   +   hydrochloric acid   →   no reaction

Non-metal and acid: no reaction

dilute acid

non-metal

Uses of metals

- Aluminium is used in aeroplanes; it has a low density and does not corrode.
- Copper is used in water pipes; it does not react with water.
- Iron is made into steel for making cookware; it is a good conductor of heat and it has a high melting point.

Uses of non-metals

- Hydrogen in rocket fuel; it has a low density and is highly inflammable.
- Oxygen for combustion, e.g. in an oxy-acetylene burner; it supports burning.

KEY FACTS

- ⬑ If an element conducts electricity it must be a metal. (But remember carbon in the form of graphite does conduct electricity.)
- ⬇ Metals form basic oxides.
- ⬇ Non-metals form acidic oxides.
- ⬆ Metals react with acids to give hydrogen.
- ➡ Non-metals do not react with acid.

EXAMINER'S TOP TIPS

Elements ending in '-ium' (e.g. sodium) are metals.

Elements ending in '-ine' (e.g. chlorine), '-gen' (e.g. oxygen) or '-on' (e.g. argon) are non-metals.

Worth their salt

Common salt (sodium chloride) was once so scarce that it was used as money. Roman soldiers received part of their pay ('salarium') in common salt. The word 'salary' is derived from the Latin word 'salarium'. The expression 'worth his salt' means that a person is competent and has worked hard and deserves his pay.

Common salt consumption

On average each one of us eats about 200 kg (over 400 lb) of salt each year. We need salt in order to live and be healthy (although too much salt is harmful). It is an essential ingredient of our diet. Although 0.28% of our weight (about 125 g) is salt, our bodies do not produce it.

There are many examples of uses of common salt in everyday life; here are just a few:

- adding flavour to food
- preventing vehicles from slipping on icy roads
- preventing build-up of limescale in dishwashers.

Making common salt

Acids are neutralised by alkalis to form a solution with a pH of 7. The products of this reaction are salt and water. Sodium chloride (common salt) is made by reacting hydrochloric acid with sodium hydroxide solution and evaporating the products to dryness. You may have tasted the salt you made.

$$\text{acid} + \underline{\text{base}} \rightarrow \text{salt} + \text{water}$$

(Remember that an alkali is a base that is soluble in water.)

Use of salts

The table gives some examples of salts together with their formulae and uses.

Salt	Formula	Use	Salt	Formula	Use
calcium sulphate	$CaSO_4$	Plaster of Paris	potassium nitrate	KNO_3	fertiliser
copper sulphate	$CuSO_4$	agriculture	sodium chloride	$NaCl$	common salt
iron sulphate	$FeSO_4$	medicine	silver nitrate	$AgNO_3$	photography
magnesium sulphate	$MgSO_4$	laxative	sodium stearate	(complex)	soap

Making salts

All salts contain metals. The second part of the name of a salt tells you what acid it is made from, e.g. chlorides are made from hydrochloric acid, sulphates from sulphuric acid and nitrates from nitric acid. This gives you clues on how to make salts.

Method 1: React a metal with an acid

Add excess metal to an acid. When no more hydrogen is given off, filter the solution. Either evaporate to dryness or, if you want crystals, evaporate until the solution becomes saturated and then leave it to cool. Examples of salts made by this method are:

zinc	+	hydrochloric acid	→	zinc chloride	+	hydrogen
magnesium	+	sulphuric acid	→	magnesium sulphate	+	hydrogen

But beware! Some metals, e.g. sodium and potassium explode when they are added to acids, so this method must not be used. Some metals, e.g. copper, silver and gold do not react with acids because they are too unreactive.

Method 2: Add an insoluble base to an acid

Heat the acid gently and then add the base. Keep stirring the mixture until no more reacts (excess base will be left). Filter and then follow in Method 1. Examples of salts made by this method are:

copper oxide	+	sulphuric acid	→	copper sulphate	+	water
lead hydroxide	+	nitric acid	→	lead nitrate	+	water

Method 3: Add a carbonate to an acid

Add excess carbonate to an acid. When no more carbon dioxide is given off, filter and then follow Method 1. Examples of salts made by this method are:

zinc carbonate	+	nitric acid	→	zinc nitrate	+	water	+	carbon dioxide
potassium carbonate	+	hydrochloric acid	→	potassium chloride	+	water	+	carbon dioxide

KEY FACTS

◁ **Metals (if they react) + acids → a salt and hydrogen.**
(Hydrogen burns with a 'pop'.)

▷ **Metal carbonates + acids → a salt + water + carbon dioxide.**
(Carbon dioxide gives a white precipitate with limewater.)

▽ **Metals + base/alkali → a salt + water.**

△ **A chemical reaction has occurred if a new substance is formed.**

EXAMINER'S TOP TIPS

Hydrochloric acid makes chlorides, sulphuric acid makes sulphates and nitric acid makes nitrates.

A balancing act

Banks use special weighing machines to count money. You have to count out the coins (say ten £2 coins) and place them in the bag. The cashier weighs them. If there was an extra £2 coin, the balance would tip in the direction of the coins and if there was a £2 coin too few, it would tip in the direction of the weight. If there were exactly ten £2 coins it would balance. Different weights are used for different coins. Forty £1 coins have the same weight as 20 £2 coins. (A 2p coin is double the weight of a 1p coin.)

In the same way chemical equations must be balanced.

IMPORTANT!

Rules for balancing chemical equations

Rule 1. You must know that the reaction takes place.

Rule 2. Write the equation in words.

Rule 3. Represent each substance by its correct symbol or formula.

Rule 4. Check that there are the same numbers of atoms on each side of the equation.

Rule 5. If the number of atoms on each side are not equal, then balance the equation by adding more atoms without altering any formulae.

Writing and balancing chemical equations

Rule	Example 1	Example 2
1	An acid (hydrochloric acid) is neutralised by an alkali (sodium hydroxide) to give a salt (sodium chloride) and water	A carbonate (calcium carbonate) reacts with an acid (hydrochloric acid) to give a salt (calcium chloride), water and carbon dioxide
2	hydrochloric acid + sodium hydroxide → sodium chloride + water	calcium oxide + hydrochloric acid → calcium chloride + water + carbon dioxide
3	$HCl + NaOH \rightarrow NaCl + H_2O$	$CaCO_3 + HCl \rightarrow CaCl_2 + H_2O + CO_2$
4	*Left-hand side:* 2 hydrogens, 1 chlorine, 1 sodium and 1 oxygen *Right-hand side:* 1 sodium, 1 chlorine, 2 hydrogens and 1 oxygen	*Left-hand side:* 1 calcium, 1 carbon, 3 oxygens, 1 hydrogen and 1 chlorine *Right-hand side:* 1 calcium, 1 carbon, 3 oxygens, 2 hydrogens and 2 chlorines
5	The two sides are equal and therefore the equation is balanced. The reaction between hydrochloric acid and sodium hydroxide is $HCl + NaOH \rightarrow NaCl + H_2O$	The hydrogen and chlorines are not equal. You need to increase (you can only increase!), the number of hydrogen atoms and chlorine atoms from 1 to 2. The equation becomes: $CaCO_3 + 2HCl \rightarrow CaCl_2 + H_2O + CO_2$ Notice the '2' goes in front of HCl. (You must **NOT** change the formula to H_2Cl_2.)

State symbols in equations

The equations in the table opposite do not tell you what state the substances are in, e.g. solid (s), liquid (l), gas (g), or dissolved in water (aq). The letters in brackets are called <u>state</u> <u>symbols</u>.

If the equation is written as:

$$H_2SO_4 \text{ (aq)} + 2NaOH \text{ (aq)} \rightarrow Na_2SO_4 \text{ (aq)} + 2H_2O \text{ (l)}$$

then we can say that dilute sulphuric acid and dilute sodium hydroxide react together to form a solution of sodium sulphate in water together with water. The equation does not tell us how fast the reaction is, or if the reaction gives out heat (<u>exothermic</u>) or takes in heat (<u>endothermic</u>).

Balancing practice

Check that the following equations are balanced.

zinc	+	hydrochloric acid	$\rightarrow$	zinc chloride	+	hydrogen
Zn (s)	+	$2HCl$ (aq)	$\rightarrow$	$ZnCl_2$ (aq)	+	H_2 (g)

magnesium	+	sulphuric acid	$\rightarrow$	magnesium sulphate	+	hydrogen
Mg (s)	+	H_2SO_4 (aq)	$\rightarrow$	$MgSO_4$ (aq)	+	H_2 (g)

copper oxide	+	nitric acid	$\rightarrow$	copper nitrate	+	water
CuO (s)	+	$2HNO_3$ (aq)	$\rightarrow$	$Cu(NO_3)_2$ (aq)	+	H_2O (l)

potassium carbonate	+	sulphuric acid	$\rightarrow$	potassium sulphate	+	carbon dioxide	+	water
K_2CO_3 (aq)	+	H_2SO_4 (aq)	$\rightarrow$	K_2SO_4 (aq)	+	CO_2 (g)	+	H_2O (l)

KEY FACTS

◁ **The number of each type of atom of reactants must equal the same number of each type of atom of products.**

▷ **Gases of elements are written as diatomic molecules (two atoms per molecule), e.g. H_2, Cl_2, O_2, N_2 but the noble gases are monatomic; they are unreactive/inert.**

EXAMINER'S TOP TIPS

There are usually two marks for writing an equation: one mark for the correct formulae and one mark for balancing the equation correctly. Make sure that you get both.

Are we tarnished for life?

Q **What do a 2p coin, a rusty nail and the dome of St Paul's Cathedral in London have in common?**

Saint Paul's dome looks green now but when it was first built it was copper coloured. In these three examples metals have reacted with air. The reactive gas in air is oxygen. The change in colour of the coin is the formation of copper oxide; rust is hydrated iron oxide and the green colour on St Paul's Cathedral is hydrated copper(II) carbonate.

This evidence suggests that metals react with oxygen and water in air (and in the case of St Paul's with carbon dioxide also).

A **They change colour because they react with substances in the air.**

Reactions of metals with oxygen

Metals react with oxygen at different rates. They act as if they are in a competition. The metals in Group 1 and Group 2 of the Periodic Table are the most reactive; the transition metals are the least reactive. When sodium and potassium are freshly cut they are very shiny but they rapidly tarnish and go dull. They have reacted with oxygen in the air to form oxides. Other metals that react rapidly with oxygen are magnesium and calcium.

If you were to study the rates of reaction of the metals:

aluminium, calcium, copper, gold, iron, lead, lithium, magnesium, platinum, potassium, silver, sodium and *zinc*

with oxygen, your results would give the following order:

potassium, sodium, lithium, calcium, magnesium, (aluminium), zinc, iron, lead, copper, silver, gold, platinum

Notice that metals ending in '-ium', e.g. magnesium, are more reactive than metals without this ending, e.g. iron.

One of the ways of remembering the order is to use a mnemonic such as:

> **Please Stop Lucy Calling My Aunt Zelda In Leeds, 'Cos She's Got Piles**

The first letter of each word is the initial letter of the metal.

Aluminium behaves differently, that is why it has been put in brackets. When it reacts with air it forms a protective oxide layer that stops it reacting further. This is why aluminium is so useful for making pots and pans used in cooking. Aluminium pans should not be used for heating acidic substances such as jams as the acid reacts with the aluminium oxide layer and makes jam poisonous.

Reactivity and the Periodic Table

The Periodic Table shows where these metals are placed. The number above each element represents the order these 11 elements appear in the <u>reactivity</u> <u>series</u>. Sodium is the most reactive and silver is the least reactive.

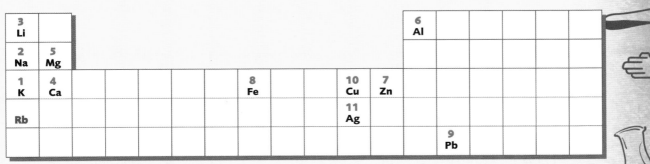

3 **Li**													**6** **Al**				
2 **Na**	**5** **Mg**																
1 **K**	**4** **Ca**							**8** **Fe**				**10** **Cu**	**7** **Zn**				
Rb												**11** **Ag**					
														9 **Pb**			

- The order of reactivity of the metals is Group 1, Group 2, Group 3 and then a random order of transition metals and lead.
- The metals get more reactive going down a group.

The metal rubidium (Rb) is shown in **blue** in the Periodic Table above. You should be able to work out that rubidium is a metal ('-ium' ending) and that it will be the most reactive out of the two metals – it is below potassium in Group 1.

Reaction of metals with water and with hydrochloric acid

The same order is obtained when these metals are reacted with water and with hydrochloric acid. The results are summarised in the table.

Metal	Reaction with water	Reaction with hydrochloric acid
K	Reacts with cold water to give hydrogen	Reacts explosively
Na	and alkali	
Li	$2Na\ (s)\ +\ 2H_2O\ (l)\ \rightarrow\ H_2\ (g)\ +\ 2NaOH\ (aq)$	
Ca		
Mg	Reacts with steam to give hydrogen and	Reacts to give hydrogen and metal chloride
Zn	metal oxide	
Fe	$Mg\ (s)\ +\ H_2O\ (g)\ \rightarrow\ H_2\ (g)\ +\ MgO\ (s)$	$Mg\ (s)\ +\ 2HCl\ (aq)\ \rightarrow\ H_2\ (g)\ +\ MgCl_2\ (aq)$
Pb		
Cu	No reaction	No reaction
Ag		

If hydrogen was added to the reactivity series it would be between lead and copper.

KEY FACTS

◁ The higher up a metal is in the reactivity series, the faster it reacts.

▷ Metals above hydrogen in the reactivity series displace hydrogen from water and hydrochloric acid.

EXAMINER'S TOP TIPS

Metals ending in '-ium', e.g. magnesium, are more reactive than metals without this ending, e.g. iron.

The power game

In any sport, one person or side is trying to win. In games such as hockey, football, netball and rugby one person is always trying to take the ball from another. A word we can use to describe the taking of something is 'displace'. A similar thing happens in chemistry. In metals one is always trying to displace another and it is always the most reactive metal that wins.

If magnesium is heated with zinc oxide, magnesium displaces the zinc to form magnesium oxide and zinc. The reaction is:

$$Mg\ (s)\ +\ ZnO\ (s)\ \rightarrow\ MgO\ (s)\ +\ Zn\ (s)$$

Zinc displaces hydrogen when heated with water (as steam). Water can also be called hydrogen oxide. The reaction is:

$$Zn\ (s)\ +\ H_2O\ (g)\ \rightarrow\ ZnO\ (s)\ +\ H_2\ (g)$$

Zinc must be more reactive than hydrogen.

Displacement reactions and reactivity series

More reactive metals will displace less reactive metals from solutions of their salts. <u>Displacement</u> <u>reactions</u> provide another way of placing metals in order of their reactivity.

	Copper sulphate	**Iron sulphate**	**Lead nitrate**	**Magnesium sulphate**
copper		No reaction	No reaction	No reaction
iron	Iron formed. Solution turns from blue to green		Lead formed. Solution changes from colourless to green	No reaction
lead	Copper formed. Solution turns from blue to colourless	No reaction		No reaction
magnesium	Copper formed. Solution turns from blue to colourless	Iron formed. Solution turns from green to colourless	Lead formed. No colour change	

If you were given this information you could work out that the most reactive metal is magnesium, followed by iron, then lead and finally copper. You could also deduce that copper sulphate solution is blue, iron sulphate solution is green and both magnesium sulphate solution and lead nitrate solution are colourless. These reactions can be represented by the equations:

$$\text{magnesium} + \text{copper sulphate} \rightarrow \text{copper} + \text{magnesium sulphate}$$
$$\text{Mg (s)} + \text{CuSO}_4\text{(aq)} \rightarrow \text{Cu (s)} + \text{MgSO}_4\text{(aq)}$$

and

$$\text{iron} + \text{lead nitrate} \rightarrow \text{lead} + \text{iron nitrate}$$
$$\text{Fe (s)} + \text{Pb(NO}_3)_2\text{ (aq)} \rightarrow \text{Pb (s)} + \text{Fe(NO}_3)_2\text{ (aq)}$$

One of the most spectacular and beautiful (but expensive) displacement reactions is that between zinc and silver nitrate. Sparkling, feather-shaped crystals of silver appear to 'grow' on the zinc. The equation for the reaction is:

$$\text{zinc} + \text{silver nitrate} \rightarrow \text{silver} + \text{zinc nitrate}$$
$$\text{Zn (s)} + \text{2AgNO}_3\text{ (aq)} \rightarrow \text{Ag (s)} + \text{Zn(NO}_3)_2\text{ (aq)}$$

All displacement reactions give out heat energy. The further apart the two metals are in the reactivity series, the greater the amount of energy given out, e.g. the reaction between magnesium and copper sulphate gives out more energy than the reaction between lead and copper sulphate.

Uses of displacement reactions

The reaction between aluminium and iron oxide is known as the <u>Thermit</u> process. It is used to weld railway lines that are made of iron. The process can be shown by the equation:

$$\text{aluminium} + \text{iron oxide} \rightarrow \text{iron} + \text{aluminium oxide}$$
$$\text{2Al (s)} + \text{Fe}_2\text{O}_3\text{ (s)} \rightarrow \text{2Fe (s)} + \text{Al}_2\text{O}_3\text{ (s)}$$

The energy from the reaction melts the railway lines. The iron formed will weld (join) any cracks in the line.

Sometimes another non-metal, carbon, is included in the series between aluminium and zinc. If carbon is heated with aluminium oxide there is no reaction. But if carbon is heated with zinc oxide, then zinc and carbon dioxide are formed as shown in the equation:

$$\text{2ZnO (s)} + \text{C (s)} \rightarrow \text{2Zn (s)} + \text{CO}_2\text{ (g)}$$

This type of reaction is very useful for manufacturing metals, particularly iron. Iron ore (iron oxide) is heated with carbon as shown in the equation:

$$\text{2Fe}_2\text{O}_3\text{ (s)} + \text{3C (s)} \rightarrow \text{4Fe (s)} + \text{3CO}_2\text{ (g)}$$

KEY FACTS

◁ **Displacement reactions of metals give the same order of reactivity as the reactions of the metals with oxygen, water and acids.**

▷ **Displacement reactions can be used for the manufacture of the less reactive metals.**

EXAMINER'S TOP TIPS

To work out the order of reactivity of metals from displacement reactions, count how many reactions take place. The metal that has the highest number of reactions is the most reactive; the metal with the least number is the least reactive.

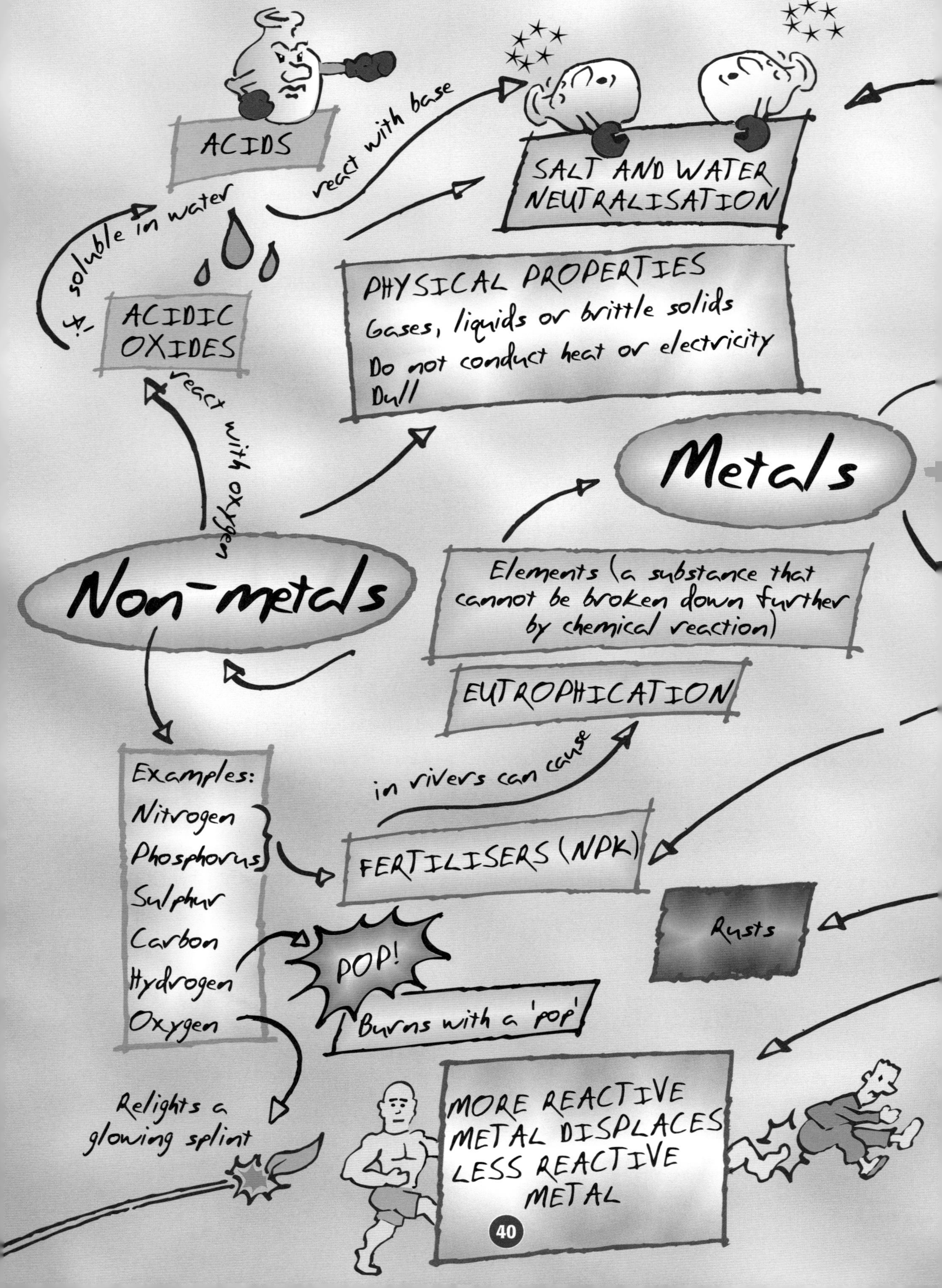

ACIDS

react with base

soluble in water

SALT AND WATER
NEUTRALISATION

ACIDIC
OXIDES

react with oxygen

PHYSICAL PROPERTIES
Gases, liquids or brittle solids
Do not conduct heat or electricity
Dull

Metals

Non-metals

Elements (a substance that
cannot be broken down further
by chemical reaction)

EUTROPHICATION

in rivers can cause

Examples:
Nitrogen
Phosphorus
Sulphur
Carbon
Hydrogen
Oxygen

FERTILISERS (NPK)

Rusts

POP!

Burns with a 'pop'

Relights a
glowing splint

MORE REACTIVE
METAL DISPLACES
LESS REACTIVE
METAL

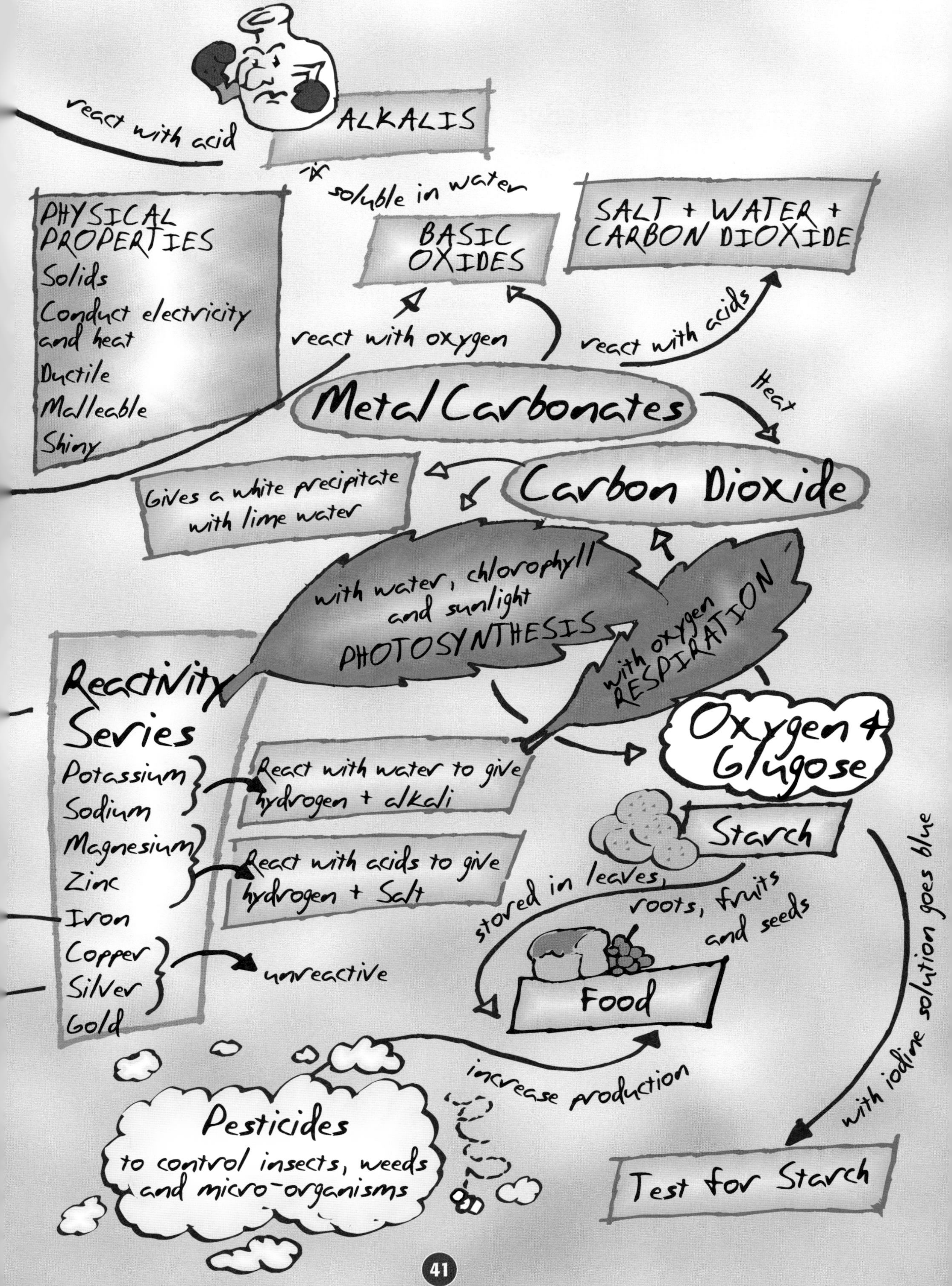

react with acid

ALKALIS

if soluble in water

PHYSICAL PROPERTIES
Solids
Conduct electricity and heat
Ductile
Malleable
Shiny

BASIC OXIDES

SALT + WATER + CARBON DIOXIDE

react with oxygen

react with acids

Metal Carbonates

Heat

Gives a white precipitate with lime water

Carbon Dioxide

with water, chlorophyll and sunlight
PHOTOSYNTHESIS

with oxygen
RESPIRATION

Reactivity Series
Potassium
Sodium
Magnesium
Zinc
Iron
Copper
Silver
Gold

React with water to give hydrogen + alkali

React with acids to give hydrogen + Salt

unreactive

Oxygen + Glucose

Starch

stored in leaves, roots, fruits and seeds

Food

increase production

Pesticides
to control insects, weeds and micro-organisms

with iodine solution goes blue

Test for Starch

Test your knowledge 2

1   The apparatus shown in the diagram can be used to prepare salts by three different methods.

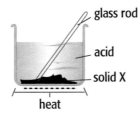

a) *Method 1*: An acid is reacted with an acid.

   (i)   Using this method, what would you react together to make magnesium sulphate?

   ....

   (ii) How would you know when the reaction had finished?

   ....

b) *Method 2*: Add a metal oxide to an acid.

   (i)   What is another name for a metal oxide?

   ....

   (ii) Which salt is made when zinc oxide reacts with nitric acid?

   ....

c) *Method 3*: Add a metal carbonate to an acid.

   (i)   Name the gas given off when a carbonate reacts with an acid.

   ....

   (ii) If the metal carbonate was soluble in water, how could you tell when all the acid had been
         used up in the reaction?

   ....

d) There is a fourth method – adding an alkali to an acid.

   (i)   What is an alkali?

   ....

   (ii) Complete the reaction:
         ACID + ALKALI → ....

                                                                                       (10 marks)

2

The diagram shows an experiment to investigate photosynthesis.

a) Name **gas X** given off during photosynthesis.

....

b) Name the TWO substances used up in photosynthesis:
   (i)   the gas obtained from air.

....

   (ii) the substance obtained from the soil.

....

c) Write the word equation for photosynthesis.

....

d) Name TWO conditions necessary for photosynthesis to take place.

   (i)   ....

   (ii) ....

(7 marks)

3   The leaf of a variegated ivy plant was partly covered by metal foil as shown
    in the diagram.

    The plant and foil were put in the dark for 24 hours. The foil was then removed
    from the plant which was then put into bright sunlight for 8 hours. After this time
    period the leaf was tested for starch. The results are as follows.

A   B   C   D

a) What is the test for starch?

....

b) (i) What would be the appearance of the leaf after testing for starch? Write either A, B, C or D.

....

   (ii) Explain your answer.

....

....

....

c) Why was the variegated ivy leaf plant left in the dark for 24 hours?

....

(7 marks)

(Total 24 marks)

Acid rain

Kilauea volcano on Big Island, Honolulu has been spewing out over 1000 tons of sulphur dioxide and other pollutants every day since 3 January 1983. This is equivalent to the pollution produced by over 3500 power stations. How would you like to live downwind of Kilauea? Most of the pollution does not hit Big Island but is instead carried by wind currents to the neighbouring island of Kono.

In addition to natural pollutants such as volcanic emissions, there are many pollutants that are man-made.

Acid rain and its effects

burning fossil fuels

emissions from power stations and factories

exhaust fumes from vehicles

carbon dioxide
carbonic acid

sulphur dioxide
sulphuric acid

oxides of nitrogen
nitric acid

Pollution builds up during the week increasing the likelihood of acid rain at the weekends. It clears over the weekend giving drier weather for the start of the new week.

ACID RAIN

Corrodes stonework and metalwork of buildings.

Destroys trees and kills animals on land and in water. It has been claimed that acid rain from factories in England is carried across the North Sea by wind to Scandinavian countries. In these countries acid rain is destroying forests and killing fish in the lakes.

Causes some people to suffer from respiratory problems, e.g. asthma because of the airborne pollutants.

Weathering

The structures shown in the photographs are nearly the same age. Cleopatra's needle was brought from Egypt and erected in London in 1879. Notice how differently they have weathered. The main cause of the accelerated weathering of Cleopatra's needle is acid rain. Calcium carbonate in building materials reacts with <u>acid rain</u>. One of the reactions taking place is:

Obelisk in Egypt

Cleopatra's needle in London

$$\text{calcium carbonate} + \text{nitric acid} \rightarrow \text{calcium nitrate} + \text{water} + \text{carbon dioxide}$$
$$CaCO_3 \text{ (s)} + 2HNO_3 \text{ (aq)} \rightarrow Ca(NO_3)_2 \text{ (aq)} + H_2O \text{ (l)} + CO_2 \text{ (g)}$$

Rain and soil pH

The distribution of plant species in the UK depends in part on the <u>pH</u> of the soil. In areas where there is a lot of rain during the summer months, soils are often acidic. Here acid-loving plants, e.g. rhododendrons, grow well. In areas where rainfall is small, the soil tends to be alkaline and acid-loving plants do not thrive.

The pH of soil is one of the most important measurements of how fertile it is. It can indicate whether a soil could:

- contain toxic levels of aluminium and manganese
- be low in bases, e.g. calcium compounds and magnesium compounds
- cause problems with uptake of essential nutrients.

Measuring pH of soil

- About 2 cm³ of soil is well shaken in about 20 cm³ of distilled water.
- The mixture is allowed to settle and then the liquid is filtered off and its pH measured using Universal Indicator paper. The pH is usually between 6.5 and 7.5. Professionals measure the pH of soil using a pH meter.

Methods of changing soil pH

Composts and manures are acidic and lower the pH of soil. To overcome this problem, a base such as lime (calcium oxide) is spread on the land. It is difficult to reduce the alkalinity of soil that has a high pH. It contains large amounts of magnesium compounds and calcium compounds. The amount of compost or manure that would have to be added would be vast, and the effect would only be short term.

Plant magic

You could try a bit of 'magic' with hydrangeas. Hydrangeas change the colour of their flowers from pink to blue, depending on the pH of the soil. It is aluminium that makes all the difference. If the soil is acidic, hydrangeas will absorb aluminium, which turns the flowers blue. If the soil is alkaline, only a very small amount of aluminium is absorbed and the flowers are pink.

Grown in alkaline soil   **Grown in acidic soil**

KEY FACTS

◄ Sulphur dioxide and oxides of nitrogen dissolve in rainwater to form acid rain.

► Acid rain destroys brickwork and metalwork.

▼ The pH of soil affects the type of plants that can grow.

EXAMINER'S TOP TIPS

Remember: Fossil fuels 'SOON' cause acid rain.
(Sulphur Oxides and Oxides of Nitrogen.)

Are we getting dirtier?

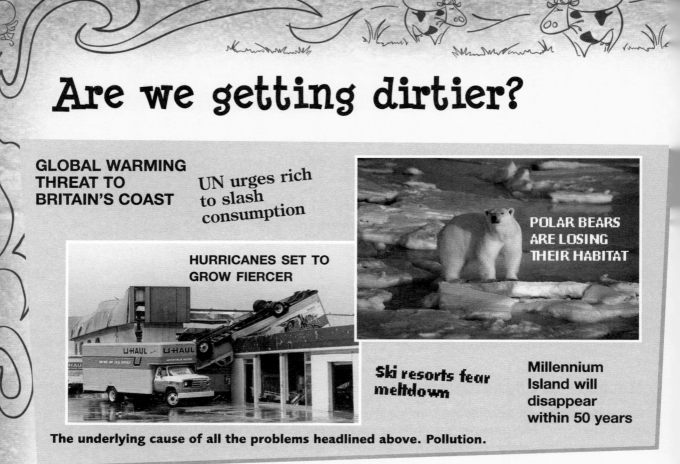

GLOBAL WARMING THREAT TO BRITAIN'S COAST

UN urges rich to slash consumption

HURRICANES SET TO GROW FIERCER

POLAR BEARS ARE LOSING THEIR HABITAT

Ski resorts fear meltdown

Millennium Island will disappear within 50 years

The underlying cause of all the problems headlined above. Pollution.

Global warming

In the last 10 000 years the average temperature of the World has risen by 4 °C. In your lifetime it is predicted to rise by another 2 °C. The effects of this seemingly small rise in temperature are thought to be extensive. Here are some of the predictions:

- Malaria will be common in the UK.
- The polar caps will be reduced considerably and the water level will rise by over 60 cm, flooding large parts of coastal England.
- We will experience severe winter floods and summer droughts.

Some of the evidence for these predictions is:

- Cases of local malaria have been found in parts of Spain.
- Since 1995, over 5400 square miles of the Antarctic ice-shelf has broken off and melted.
- There have been more severe storms and droughts throughout the World.

Greenhouse effect

The greenhouse effect is the rise in temperature of the Earth because of certain gases in the atmosphere, especially carbon dioxide and methane, which trap energy from the Sun. Without these gases, heat would escape back into Space. The greenhouse effect is important; without it the Earth would not be warm enough for humans to live. Without the effect the average temperature would be about 30 °C colder than at present.

radiated heat energy

heat from the Sun

trapped heat reflected back

atmosphere

Ozone layer

Do not confuse the greenhouse effect with the hole in the ozone layer. The ozone layer in the upper atmosphere prevents over-exposure to ultraviolet radiations that can cause skin cancer and eye diseases, e.g. cataracts. The radiations can also harm plants and animals.

The hole in the ozone layer (shown in dark blue) in the photograph causes more ultraviolet rays to reach the surface of the Earth. The hole is caused by chlorofluorocarbons (CFCs). Chlorofluorocarbons are found in aerosols, older type refrigerators and certain cleaning solvents. The CFCs destroy the ozone layer by a series of complex reactions making the layer thinner until a hole is formed.

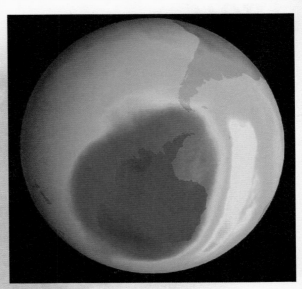

Reducing pollution

Scientists have come up with strategies to reduce the effects of pollution. Some of them are listed below.

- Catalytic converters are put in modern cars. These convert the oxides of nitrogen to the harmless gas nitrogen.

- Chimneys in power stations are lined with a basic oxide, e.g. calcium oxide. Calcium oxide neutralises the acidic gases.

- The use of CFCs has been banned and alternatives used in aerosols and refrigerators.

- The Clean Air Act in 1993 made it an offence to cause or permit emissions of 'dark smoke' from industrial or trade premises. It also enables local authorities to declare any part of its district as a 'smoke control area'.

KEY FACTS

◁ The greenhouse effect is caused by certain gases in the atmosphere such as carbon dioxide.

▷ Holes in the ozone layer are caused by CFCs.

Fuels

I am a fuel. Which fuel am I?

- I can be made from water.
- I make no polluting gases.
- I make only water when burned.
- I am the most abundant element on Earth.
- I would make every nation self-sufficient in energy.
- I could stop oil-price wars (and possibly warfare).
- I am expensive and difficult to store.

The answer is hydrogen.

North Sea gas (methane)

Methane gas is a <u>fuel</u>. A fuel is a substance that burns easily to produce heat and light. Pure methane has no smell, but strong smelling dimethyl sulphide or tertiary butyl mercaptan is added so leaks can be detected. The substances added are called 'stenching agents'. Methane is a dangerous gas.

- Although it is not poisonous, inhaling excess methane can suffocate (asphyxiate) a person.
- It catches fire easily.
- If a sufficiently large amount escapes, it can explode.

Carbon monoxide detectors

If there is insufficient ventilation in a house, methane does not burn completely and produces a very poisonous gas called carbon monoxide. Carbon monoxide has no smell so it is impossible to detect unless there is a carbon monoxide detector in the home. Every home that uses gas should fit a carbon monoxide detector. There are two types; one produces a colour change and the other sets off an alarm.

When methane burns **completely** in air the reaction is:

methane	+	oxygen	→	carbon dioxide	+	water
CH_4 (g)	+	$2O_2$ (g)	→	CO_2 (g)	+	$2H_2O$ (g)

When methane burns **incompletely** in air the reaction is:

methane	+	oxygen	→	carbon monoxide	+	water
$2CH_4$ (g)	+	$3O_2$ (g)	→	$2CO$ (g)	+	$4H_2O$ (g)

Carbon monoxide burns with a blue flame to give carbon dioxide. The blue flame in fires is carbon monoxide gas burning. The danger sign is if the colour of the flame goes yellow. This means that carbon monoxide is being formed due to incomplete combustion.

Other fuels

There are many other fuels; they can be gases, liquids or solids:

- gaseous fuels, e.g. methane, butane
- liquid fuels, e.g. petrol, diesel
- solids, e.g. wood, coal.

All these fuels contain carbon and hydrogen and burn completely to give carbon dioxide and water.

Matches

Matches have a short wooden stick with a small head coloured red or black. The head is made of a compound called potassium chlorate ($KClO_3$) and the elements sulphur and carbon. Sometimes a colouring agent is added, such as the red colour in the photograph. The striking surface on the matchbox is made of powdered glass and red phosphorus. The friction between the match and the box produces sufficient heat to cause the phosphorus to ignite. This ignition starts the combustion of the match head. Potassium chlorate contains oxygen and helps the sulphur and carbon to burn. The burning sulphur then sets light to the wooden stick. The familiar smell when matches are lit is a mixture of phosphorus oxides and sulphur dioxide.

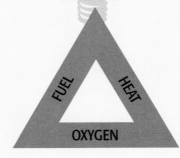

Keep the fire burning

Heat, fuel and oxygen are necessary for making and maintaining a fire. The fire will go out:

- if there is not enough heat generated to keep the fire burning
- when the fuel is used up, removed or isolated
- when the oxygen supply is limited or removed.

KEY FACTS

- ⬆ **A fuel is a substance that burns in air (oxygen) to produce light and heat energy.**
- ➡ **If a fuel contains carbon and hydrogen the products will include carbon dioxide and water.**
- ⬇ **Carbon monoxide is a poisonous gas formed by the incomplete combustion of fossil fuels.**

EXAMINER'S TOP TIPS

The fire triangle shows the three things that must be present for a fire to burn.

FUEL   HEAT

OXYGEN

Energising facts

Max has accidentally bitten on a piece of aluminium foil and has felt a sharp pain in his mouth. He gets the pain because he has metal fillings in some of his teeth. He has set up a simple cell (battery). The aluminium metal (in the foil) and the mercury or gold metal in his fillings and the saliva in his mouth (the <u>electrolyte</u>) makeup the cell. The voltage produced by the cell is about 2.5 V.

Batteries

Billions of batteries are sold every year. Some batteries can be recharged and most batteries can be recycled.

If you read the labelling on the outside of a battery you will see:

* + (positive terminal) and − (negative terminal) signs
* instructions in several languages on how to dispose of the battery
* the type of battery AA, AAA, C etc.
* the voltage it will produce.

But there is no indication of the names of the substances inside it. There are two basic chemicals: elements and an electrolyte (either an acid, <u>alkali</u> or a salt).

Simple batteries

The early batteries were based on two metals and an electrolyte. In theory any chemical reaction that gives out heat energy can be used to make a battery.

There is a scientific law that states 'Energy cannot be created or destroyed, but it can be converted into other types of energy'. In batteries chemical energy is converted into electrical energy.

When zinc and copper are dipped into dilute sulphuric acid a <u>simple cell</u> is made. The voltmeter, V, will read 1.1 V. The zinc rod reacts with sulphuric acid to form zinc sulphate and hydrogen. Small bubbles of hydrogen gas form at the copper rod.

The further apart the two metals are in the reactivity series, the greater the voltage produced between them. Magnesium and silver produce a voltage of 3.17 V between them. Copper and silver can only produce a voltage of 0.46 V between them. Rods made of the same metal produce no voltage.

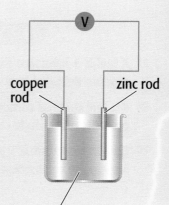

copper rod   zinc rod

dilute sulphuric acid

Exothermic and endothermic reactions

You may remember when you studied displacement reactions involving metals that the reaction mixture warmed up, e.g. when zinc is added to copper sulphate solution the temperature rises by about 3 °C. The reaction gives out heat energy: it is called an exothermic reaction. Most reactions are exothermic, but some, e.g. the reaction between citric acid and sodium hydrogencarbonate take in heat energy, they are called endothermic reactions.

Using exothermic reactions

Rusting of iron is an exothermic reaction. It is a very slow reaction and hence we do not notice the heat change. Rusting can be used as a chemical heater. Iron filings, magnesium powder and sodium chloride are mixed together and kept in a dry container. When heat is required to heat up food or to keep you warm, water is added to the mixture. After a few seconds the temperature rises to the boiling point of water and it is ready to use. Climbers and people travelling in very cold countries use this method to heat food and for keeping warm.

Other uses of chemicals in everyday life

There is a vast range of materials made by chemical reactions; some examples are given in the list.

- Fertilisers, e.g. all inorganic fertilisers.
- Materials for buildings, e.g. cement, concrete, bricks.
- Most medicines, e.g. aspirin, insulin, iron sulphate.
- Plastics, e.g. nylon, rayon, PVC, terylene, bakelite, Teflon.
- Soaps and detergents, e.g. natural oils are reacted with sodium hydroxide or sulphuric acid.
- Vitamins, most can be made synthetically.

And there are chemical reactions that occur in nature, e.g. photosynthesis and respiration.

photosynthesis:	carbon dioxide + water →	glucose + oxygen
respiration:	glucose + oxygen →	carbon dioxide + water

KEY FACTS

⬆ **In a cell the most reactive metal is always the negative electrode.**

➡ **Reactions that give out energy are called exothermic reactions.**

⬇ **Reactions that absorb energy are called endothermic reactions.**

⬆ **Energy cannot be created or destroyed.**

⬅ **Many important everyday substances are made by chemical reactions.**

EXAMINER'S TOP TIPS

Remember: 'Ex' means 'out' as in exit. An exothermic reaction gives out heat energy.

Here to stay

'MATTER CANNOT BE CREATED OR DESTROYED.'

'The sum of the masses of the reactants is always equal to the sum of the masses of the products.'

Proving the law using chemical reactions

Choose a reaction where a chemical change takes place. In a <u>chemical</u> <u>reaction</u> a new substance is formed and there is an energy change. The reaction between copper sulphate and zinc is shown below.

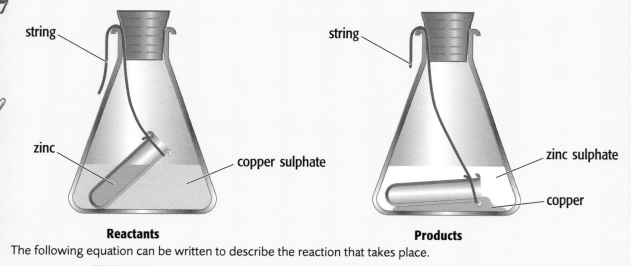

Reactants

Products

The following equation can be written to describe the reaction that takes place.

zinc	+	copper sulphate	→	copper	+	zinc sulphate
Zn (s)	+	$CuSO_4$ (aq)	→	Cu (s)	+	$ZnSO_4$ (aq)

In this reaction:

• there is a colour change from blue to colourless
• a brown precipitate of copper is formed
• there is a rise in temperature.

An experiment is set up so that the reactants can be kept separate and accurately weighed at the start of the reaction. The reactants are then mixed and the products are accurately weighed at the end of the experiment. The two weights are then compared. They will be the same.

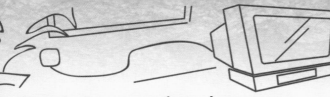

Burning magnesium in oxygen

When magnesium burns in air its mass increases. It reacts with oxygen in the air to form magnesium oxide. You may have seen a series of experiments in which different masses of magnesium are burned in air and the product (magnesium oxide) is weighed. The readings taken are:

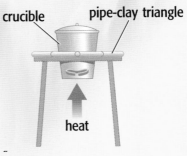

crucible   pipe-clay triangle

heat

Mass of crucible at start $= x\,g$
Mass of crucible + magnesium $= y\,g$
Mass of crucible + magnesium oxide $= z\,g$

From these results:

mass of magnesium used $= (y - x)\,g$
mass of magnesium oxide formed $= (z - x)\,g$

The results of a class experiment of burning magnesium in air are shown in the table and on the graph.

Mass of magnesium/g	Mass of magnesium oxide/g
1.0	1.7
2.0	3.6
3.0	5.0
4.0	7.0
5.0	7.8
6.0	10.0

From the results it can be seen that as the mass of magnesium increases, the mass of magnesium oxide increases. It is possible to make predictions from the graph. The mass of magnesium oxide formed from 1.5 g of magnesium would be 2.5 g. So the mass formed from 15.0 g of magnesium would be 25.0 g.

The equation for the reaction is:

magnesium + oxygen → magnesium oxide

$2Mg\,(s) + O_2(g) \rightarrow 2MgO\,(s)$

In the diagram atoms of magnesium and oxygen are shown as coloured circles and they have been put on an 'atomic balance'. We can see that there is a rearrangement of atoms – atoms are not lost or gained during a chemical reaction.

KEY FACTS

1. Matter cannot be created or destroyed in a chemical reaction; the mass of the products equals the mass of the reactants.

2. Therefore atoms cannot be created or destroyed in a chemical reaction.

EXAMINER'S TOP TIPS

Count the number of atoms on each side of an equation and make sure they are equal.

Energy for life

Using the table below, identify the different types of <u>energy</u> shown in the picture. Once you have found the example in the picture, tick it off in the table. Which type of energy is missing from the picture?

Type of energy	Example	Notes
CHEMICAL	Box of matches	Chemical energy is the energy stored in a substance. The energy is released during a chemical reaction.
ELECTRICAL	Electrical equipment	Electrical energy is the most useful form of energy. Electric currents have energy. Electrical energy is easily converted into other forms of energy.
HEAT or THERMAL	Coal fire	Heat energy moves from a place of higher temperature to one of lower temperature. Normally it is colder the higher the altitude.
KINETIC	Running	Anything that moves has kinetic energy (KE). The greater the speed of an object, the greater its kinetic energy. If two objects have the same speed, the larger object has the larger kinetic energy.
LIGHT	Light bulb	Anything that is luminous gives off light energy. Light enables us to see things; it comes mainly from the Sun. Examples of luminous objects include torches, light bulbs and candles.
NUCLEAR	Atom bomb	Nuclear energy is released when atoms are split – nuclear fission, or when atoms join together – nuclear fusion.
POTENTIAL	Diving	Potential energy is the energy a body has because of its position. There are two forms: gravitational and elastic. Gravitational depends on how high an object is; elastic depends on the arrangement in the object, e.g. a wound-up clock spring, or when the elastic is pulled on a catapult.
SOUND	Radio	Your parents might complain about the sound energy coming from your room. Sound energy can be detected with our ears. Vibrations cause it. Sound waves travel through the air.

What is energy?

Energy helps you to function. It is energy that helps you to move around. You obtain that energy from the food you eat.

Energy, like matter, cannot be created or destroyed, but it can be converted from one form to another. All energy eventually ends up as heat energy and therefore, as we use energy, so the world is getting gradually warmer.

Energy conversions

Some possible energy conversions are shown in the diagram. A few examples will explain how energy is transferred.

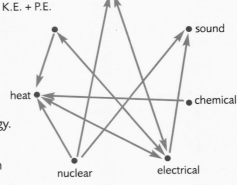

- If you were to touch a light bulb when it was on, you would find it is very hot (don't try it!). Electrical energy → light energy and heat energy.

- If you wind up a clockwork toy that has wheels and let it go, it will shoot across the room. Potential energy → kinetic energy and some sound energy.

- One of the fuels used in Space exploration is hydrogen. When a rocket is launched, oxygen is added to hydrogen and the mixture ignited. Chemical energy → kinetic energy, light energy and sound energy.

- Photosynthesis cannot take place without sunlight. Light energy → chemical energy.

Source of energy

The source of almost any form of energy can be traced back to the Sun. An example is shown below.

energy from the Sun → chemical energy in coal → heat energy from burning coal → kinetic engine of turbine rotating → electrical energy → heat from elements in electric fire

EXAMINER'S TOP TIPS

Remember: 'SPECKLE HEN' will give you the different forms of energy.

Sound; Potential; Electrical; Chemical; Kinetic; Light (energy); Heat (energy); Nuclear

KEY FACTS

➔ Energy cannot be created or destroyed, but it can be converted from one form to another.

⬇ All energy eventually ends up as heat energy.

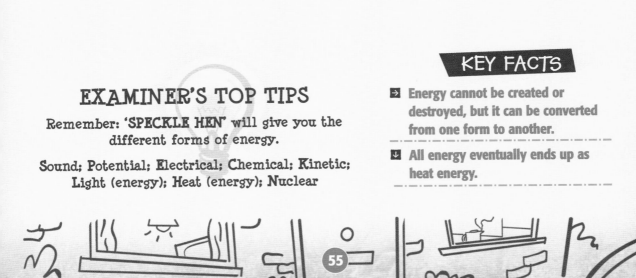

Passing through

TRUE STORY!

A bird dropped a snake over a Californian power station, short-circuiting a line and causing a two-hour blackout.

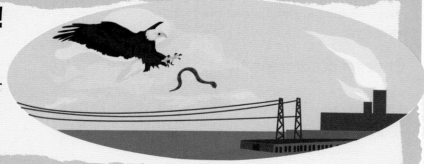

If this were to happen where you live, it is improbable that everybody's electricity in the area would be affected. The power supply is split into three circuits, called phases. The same is true within houses and within appliances.

Circuits

How many electrical appliances do you have on your downstairs mains ring circuit? You could have some of the following: a television, sound system, microwave, kettle, toaster, washing machine, tumble dryer and computer.

You know that there are two types of circuits – series and parallel.

In the circuits shown below the bulbs, ammeters, battery and wire are identical. An ammeter measures the size of an electric current in amperes (A). Ammeters are always connected in series in a circuit.

Series circuit

3A
3A
1.5A
1.5A
1A
1A
Bulbs get dimmer

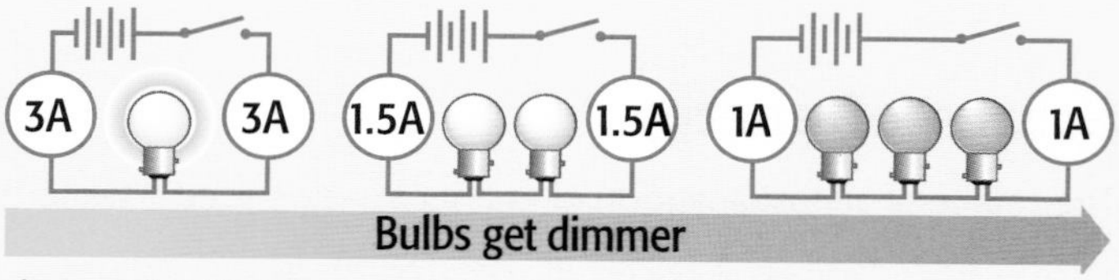

- For each series circuit, the current going into the bulbs is the same as the current coming out.
- The more bulbs that there are in the circuit the smaller the current. Adding more bulbs increases the resistance in the circuit and the bulbs get dimmer.

Parallel circuit

- The current going through each bulb is the same for each parallel circuit.
- The sum of the current through the bulbs is equal to the total current in the circuit. The bulbs have the same brightness.

Increasing the number of cells in a battery also increases the brightness of the bulbs. The greater the voltage produced by the battery, the greater the current going round the circuit.

In both circuits the current is not used up. How do bulbs produce light? The current in the circuit transfers energy from the battery to the bulbs. The electrical energy is changed into light energy and heat energy.

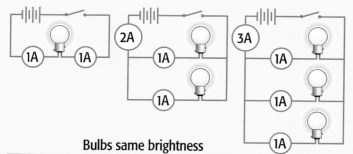

1A
1A
2A
1A
1A
3A
1A
1A
1A
Bulbs same brightness

A model to explain transfer of energy

A watering system for a garden can be used to explain how energy is transferred and why the current remains constant. Note that the water circuit has to be complete.

- The water pump is equivalent to a battery. The pump drives the water around the pipes and supplies nutrients.

- The tap is the switch – it has to be turned on for the water to flow.

- The pipe is the wire – the change in diameter of the pipe and the plants growing is equivalent to the different resistances (components, e.g. light bulbs) in the circuit. The narrower the tube is the greater will be its resistance.

The tap is turned on and water carrying the nutrients flows round the circuit. Where the pipe is narrow it is more difficult for the water to flow. At these points, where the plants are growing, nutrients pass from water to the plants. By the time the water gets back to the pump, all the nutrients have been used up, so more nutrients (energy) have to be added.

In your house, energy is transferred round the circuit by moving charged particles called electrons. As charged particles move around a circuit they gain energy from the battery and give it to the components.

Nutrients in   Tap

water pump

Voltmeters

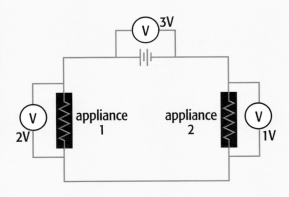

The diagram shows <u>voltmeters</u> being used to measure the volts across an appliance. Voltmeters are always connected in parallel with the power supply or appliance.

- In a series circuit: the sum of the voltages across each appliance equals the voltage supplied by the power supply.
- In a parallel circuit: the voltage across each appliance is the same as that of the power supply.

KEY FACTS

↑ **In an electric circuit ammeters are connected in series and voltmeters are connected in parallel.**

→ **The greater the resistance in a circuit, the smaller the current.**

↓ **Increasing the voltage increases the current.**

EXAMINER'S TOP TIPS

Learn how to draw circuits in series and circuits in parallel. In a circuit, voltmeters are always connected in parallel; and ammeters are always connected in series.

Warming up

'Imagine most of our reserves in the North Sea have been used up. Britain is struggling to generate enough electricity to cope with demand. The UK is heavily dependent on imported gas from Russia to generate electricity. A terrorist attack on a gas pipeline in Russia has a disastrous effect on Britain.

Immediately whole sections of the country begin to lose power. Very quickly the south-east of England is plunged into darkness; householders are left with no water or electricity; traffic is gridlocked, tube trains are stranded underground and airports closed.

As the situation worsens emergency services are affected and people's lives put at risk.'

This scenario was actually the basis of a fictional TV documentary called 'If ... the Lights Go Out'. It was set in 2010s Britain.

Power stations

Electricity is made (generated) in power stations. There are two main types of power stations:

- <u>fossil</u> <u>fuel</u>
- nuclear.

A small amount of electricity is made using renewable resources such as the Sun and wind. In the UK most of our electricity is generated from fossil fuels.

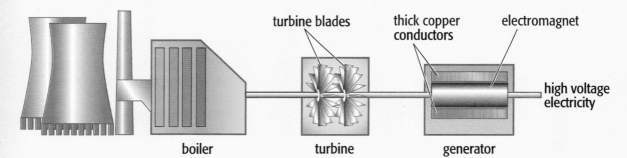

Coal-fired power station

Fossil fuel power stations and nuclear power stations both produce energy in the same way but they use different sources of energy.

- Fossil fuel stations burn fossil fuels, e.g. coal or oil.
- Nuclear power stations produce energy by splitting the nuclei of uranium atoms (<u>nuclear</u> <u>fission</u>) into smaller ones.

Nuclear power station

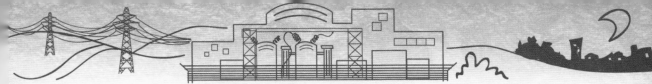

Fossil fuels vs nuclear power

Advantages

Fossil fuel power station	Nuclear power station
Gives a large amount of energy from a small amount of fuel	Does not produce smoke or carbon dioxide, so it does not contribute to the greenhouse effect
Readily available – if more energy is needed, more fuel is burned	Produces small amounts of waste

Disadvantages

Non-renewable	Non-renewable
Causes pollution by burning to give carbon dioxide, sulphur dioxide and smoke	Waste produced is very dangerous (it is sealed up and buried for many years)
Water used as coolant and may be returned as warm water into rivers. (Hot water reduces the amount of oxygen in rivers)	Very expensive to build (a lot of money has to be spent on automatic safety systems)

The Chernobyl disaster gave nuclear power stations a bad name. The engineers there turned off the automatic safety system. That cannot happen to nuclear power stations in the UK.

Energy efficiency

Many people still use traditional (incandescent) bulbs around the house. These generate light by passing an electric current through a thin metal wire, which becomes hot and emits light. Only 10% of the electrical energy is converted to light – 90% is wasted as heat energy. Energy-saver lamps are more efficient than incandescent bulbs because most of the electrical energy is used to generate light, instead of heat. Energy-saver lamps also last longer.

Traditional light bulb   **Energy-saver light bulb**

Sankey diagrams

energy as light 10%

electrical energy 100%

energy as heat 90%

Energy transfer can be shown using Sankey diagrams. These show the energy that is useful and the energy that is dissipated and not useful. The diagram shows how inefficient the energy transfer for the incandescent lamp is.

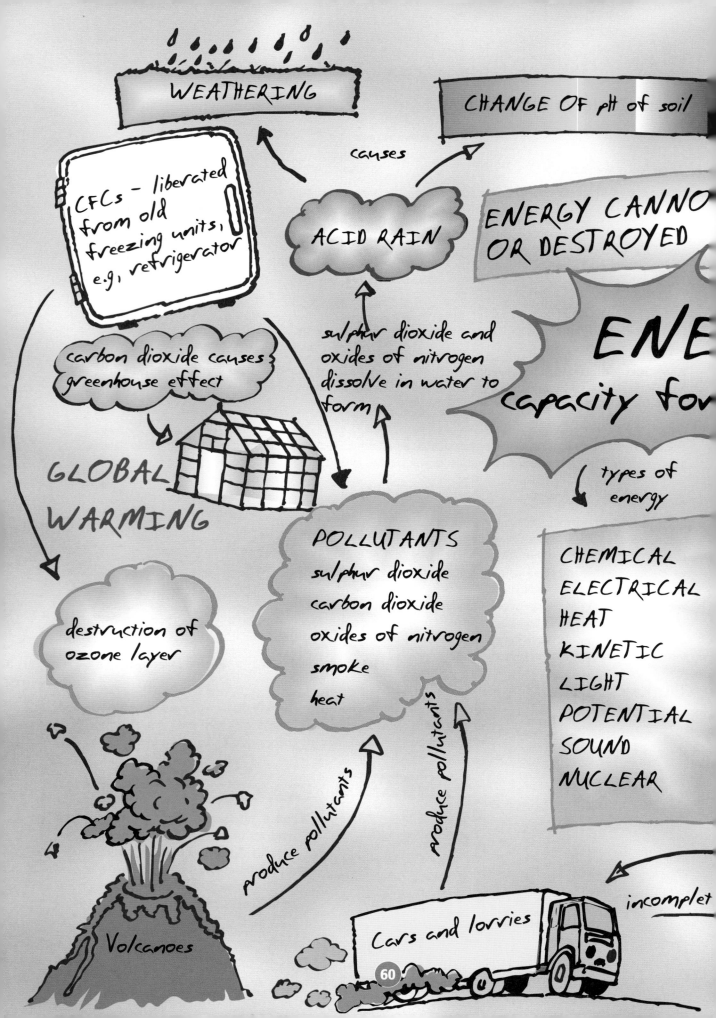

WEATHERING

CHANGE OF pH of soil

CFCs - liberated from old freezing units, e.g, refrigerator

carbon dioxide causes greenhouse effect

causes

ACID RAIN

ENERGY CANNO
OR DESTROYED

ENE

sulphur dioxide and oxides of nitrogen dissolve in water to form

capacity for

GLOBAL
WARMING

types of energy

destruction of ozone layer

POLLUTANTS
sulphur dioxide
carbon dioxide
oxides of nitrogen
smoke
heat

CHEMICAL
ELECTRICAL
HEAT
KINETIC
LIGHT
POTENTIAL
SOUND
NUCLEAR

produce pollutants

produce pollutants

incomplet

Volcanoes

Cars and lorries

fast rusting is used as a source of HEAT

ENDOTHERMIC

EXOTHERMIC

take in energy

give out energy

electrical energy

heat energy converted to

3E CREATED

RGY

loing work

CHEMICAL REACTIONS

BATTERY

ELECTRICITY

POWER STATIONS

FUELS
Coal
Oil
Petrol
Diesel

circuits can be arranged in

SERIES

PARALLEL

Used for

incomplete combustion

necessary for burning

ombustion

CARBON MONOXIDE
no smell
highly poisonous

Air

Heat

Fuel

Test your knowledge 3

1   A student was studying the reaction of zinc with copper sulphate. The apparatus and zinc and copper sulphate solution were weighed and the temperature of the mixture taken. Zinc was added to the copper sulphate solution, the mixture stirred and the highest temperature reached was recorded. The apparatus and products were weighed at the end of the experiment.

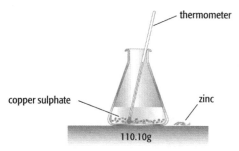

The following results were obtained:

Colour of solution at start	blue
Colour of solution at finish	colourless + brown solid
Temperature of copper sulphate at start	25.1 °C
Temperature of copper sulphate at end of experiment	28.2 °C
Mass of zinc and copper sulphate at start	110.10 g
Mass of products at the end of the experiment	110.10 g

a) (i)   Name the brown solid formed.

....

(ii) What is the change in temperature? ....

(iii) State, with a reason, whether the reaction is exothermic or endothermic.

....

b) Describe or draw a piece of apparatus to show how electrical energy can be obtained from this experiment instead of heat energy.

(7 marks)

2   A steam train burns coal to heat up water in the boiler. Coal is carried in a special container behind the train called a tender. The coal is shovelled into the fire by a stoker. The water turns to steam. The steam pushes the pistons on the wheels and the train moves. When the train approaches a tunnel, the driver puts on the lights and pulls a lever and a whistle blows.

a) In the energy transfer diagram on the facing page what should be written at **A, B** and **C**?

```
                    coal burning
                    in air                              ┌──────────┐
┌──────────────┐                    ┌──────────┐        │    B     │         ┌──────────┐
│ chemical     │    ───────────▶    │    A     │        └──────────┘         │          │
│ energy       │                    │          │        ───────────▶         │    C     │
└──────────────┘                    └──────────┘                             └──────────┘
```

A ....

B ....

C ....

b) Name TWO other forms of energy mentioned in the introduction that are obtained from
   burning coal.

   (i)   ....

   (ii)   ....

c) About 30% of the energy from coal is turned into energy to move the train. What form of energy
   accounts for the major loss of energy?

   ....

d) Coal contains sulphur. Name two pollutants that might be formed when coal burns in the
   steam engine.

   (i)   ....

   (ii)   ....

e) Apart from pollution, suggest a reason why steam trains were replaced by electric trains.

   ....

                                                                                       (10 marks)

3 Match the human activity (column A) with its effects (column B). Each item in column A can be
   matched with more than one item in column B. One has been done for you.

Activities (column A)   **Effect (column B)**

A Burying too much rubbish that   •   •   1 Buildings will be damaged
   releases poisonous chemicals into
   the soil

B Cutting down forests on a large scale •   •   2 Fossil fuels will run out

C Over-hunting of wild animals   •   •   3 Water supplies will be polluted

D Releasing too much sulphur dioxide   •   •   4 Human beings will lose a valuable
   into the atmosphere   source of natural drugs

E Using coal, oil and gas at a very   •   •   5 Wildlife will become extinct
   fast rate

                                                                                        (7 marks)

                                                                                (Total 24 marks)
```
```

The big attraction

'Houston, we have a problem.' These words were spoken by James Lovell on 13 April 1970. Lovell and two other astronauts were over 200 000 miles from Earth (320 000 kilometres) in Apollo 13 when an explosion ruptured an oxygen tank in the service module. There was a major shortage of power and oxygen – the Moon mission had to be abandoned. But how were the astronauts to return?

The answer was gravity. Apollo 13's crew changed its course and, using the Moon's gravity, managed to swing round the Moon. Using the Earth's gravity, and the small amount of power left on board they managed to return safely to Earth on 17 April .

Lovell had feared that he and his crew would end up circling in Space for ever. It has since been shown that if the correction to the flight path had not been made the spacecraft would have crashed into the Earth 35 days later. In those 35 days, the craft would have orbited the Earth and Moon three times.

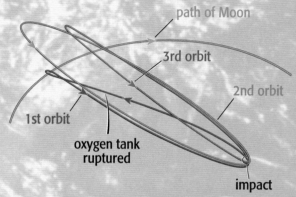

path of Moon

3rd orbit

2nd orbit

1st orbit

oxygen tank ruptured

impact

The diagram shows the three orbits in different colours. The astronauts only had sufficient supplies of oxygen to keep them alive for a maximum of ten days after the accident.

Gravity

Ask anyone who discovered <u>gravity</u> and they will say 'Newton'. In fact Newton did not discover gravity; it was there all the time. But the apple falling on his head made him think; he explained gravity by stating that all masses attract one another. The larger the mass the larger will be its attractive force (gravity). The apple, being a small mass, was attracted to the larger mass, Earth. In the case of Apollo 13, we can see in the diagram that the Earth's force of gravity on the spacecraft is much larger than that of the Moon.

Launching a rocket

For a rocket to leave Earth, the thrust developed by its engines must be greater than the downward force exerted by the weight of the rocket. (It also has to overcome air resistance.) The heavier the rocket, the more fuel is required to thrust the rocket into Space.

To help overcome this problem, scientists have built the rocket engines in stages on top of one another.

- The first engine (booster) is the most powerful and as soon as its fuel is used up (after about two minutes), it is jettisoned.
- The fuel in engine two then ignites. Less energy is required since the rocket weighs less and the rocket moves faster.
- Finally the stage two rocket is jettisoned and the stage three rocket takes over.

Weightlessness and free fall

When you see films or videos of astronauts floating, they are NOT in zero gravity. They are in a state of 'free fall', rather like skydivers. Attaching a weight to a forcemeter and dropping it can show this effect. The <u>forcemeter</u> will read zero.

Gravity and distance

Gravity depends not only on mass but also on distance. The further away two masses are, the smaller the attraction between them.

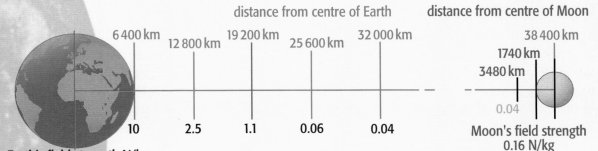

distance from centre of Earth

distance from centre of Moon

The greater the distance from the Earth, the smaller the strength of the gravity field. You can calculate that doubling the distance from the centre of the Earth reduces the gravity field by a quarter and trebling the distance the gravity field by a ninth.

Assuming James Lovell had a mass of 72 kg, he would have weighed 720 <u>newtons</u> on Earth and only 120 newtons on the Moon.

If the Earth decreased to the size of the Moon (the Moon is about 3.7 times smaller than the Earth), the Earth's gravity would be 14 times larger. Lovell would now weigh 10 080 newtons. Life would be very different! But he would still have the same mass.

KEY FACTS

⬆ **Earth's gravity pulls objects towards the centre of the Earth.**

➡ **Gravity depends upon masses of objects and the distances between the objects.**

⬇ **Free fall causes 'weightlessness' of astronauts.**

EXAMINER'S TOP TIPS

There must be two masses in order for there to be gravity. The larger mass has the greater attraction.

Keep on moving

The Solar System

Historically, there have been two main theories about our Solar System:

Ptolemy   **Galileo**

- the heliocentric system, in which the Sun is assumed to be at the centre of the Solar System
- the geocentric system, in which the Earth is assumed to be the centre of the Solar System.

The earliest recorded theory was that the Earth and the planets revolved around the Sun. This was proposed in about 500 BC. The theory could not explain why the stars remained in the same positions despite the Earth's changing viewpoints as it moved around the Sun.

In the second century AD, Ptolemy put forward his theory that this anomaly could be explained if the Earth was in a fixed position and the Sun and planets moved around the Earth. The theory held for the next 1400 years until Copernicus, and later Galileo, proved that we did live in a heliocentric system. Galileo was imprisoned in 1633 by the Spanish Inquisition for daring to state that the Earth was not the centre of the Universe.

Our Solar System

- Everything is moving in Space. In our <u>Solar</u> <u>System</u> planets, comets and asteroids go around the <u>Sun</u>. <u>Moons</u> go around the <u>planets</u>. The Sun makes up 99.85% of all the matter in our Solar System.
- Our Solar System travels in an orbit around the centre of our <u>galaxy</u> (the Milky Way) at a speed of a few hundred kilometres per second. The Milky Way is a spiral disk of 200 billion stars (one of which is our Sun).
- It takes our Solar System about 230 million years to complete one orbit around the centre of the Milky Way. The Solar System is moving at about 20 kilometres per second with respect to the nearby stars. It is heading outwards from the centre of the Milky Way.
- Our galaxy, which is one of billions of galaxies known, is travelling through intergalactic Space at a velocity of several hundred kilometres per second.
- We are still making new discoveries. In 2004 astronomers detected what could be the Solar System's tenth planet. They have named it Sedna.

What keeps the planets in orbit?

A hammer thrower has a weight at the end of a long chain. He whirls the chain in a circle before letting go of it. What happens? At first the chain remains taut. The force towards the hammer thrower is the same as the outward force. As soon as he lets go of the hammer it flies off into the field. Planets behave in a similar way. The hammer thrower is the Sun; the ball is one of the planets and the inward force is gravity. If the gravitational force could be turned off, the planets would fly off into Space.

Orbits

The planets move round the Sun in <u>orbits</u>. The orbits of Mercury and Pluto are ellipses. The orbits of all the other planets are very nearly circles. The distance between the Earth and the Sun does not change very much during the year. Because Mercury and Pluto move in ellipses, the speed at which they travel around the Sun varies. The closer these planets are to the Sun, the faster they travel.

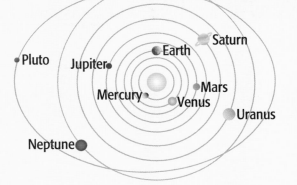

Satellites

The Moon is a natural <u>satellite</u> of the Earth. It is the gravity of the Earth that keeps the Moon in orbit. There are also artificial (man-made) satellites orbiting the Earth.

- Communication satellites. Satellites are used to send overseas phone calls or to beam TV channels into your home. They work non-stop, all-day and every day to keep the entire world linked. You only have to look around you to see the number of satellite dishes on houses. Communication satellites have to be <u>geostationary</u>. This means that they rotate at the same speed and in the same direction as the Earth, and therefore remain in the same position over a place on Earth. Satellite dishes point in a fixed direction to maintain links with a satellite.
- Weather satellites. These take photographs of the Earth at regular intervals. The photographs help weather forecasters to predict changes in weather. If you are on the Internet you are able to see these photographs. You can check what the weather is like at your holiday destination.
- Astronomy satellites. These are mounted on Earth-orbiting satellites or on deep-Space probes. They have a very clear view of Space because the light they receive does not have to pass through the Earth's atmosphere. The Hubble telescope has taken some fantastic views of stars and galaxies. The photograph shows a star being born.

There are many other uses of satellites, e.g. spying, and helping aircraft, cars and ships navigate.

KEY FACTS

➡ Objects always fall to the centre of a planet.

➡ Gravity is the force acting between any two masses pulling them together.

➡ The Sun's gravitational pull keeps the planets in orbit.

➡ The Earth's gravitational pull keeps the Moon in orbit.

EXAMINER'S TOP TIPS

Satellites can be seen because they reflect light. When there is an eclipse of the Moon, the Moon goes into the shadow of the Earth. Do not say that the Earth goes in front of the Moon or that the Earth gets in the way.

Moving fast

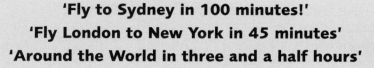

'Fly to Sydney in 100 minutes!'
'Fly London to New York in 45 minutes'
'Around the World in three and a half hours'

It is confidently predicted that aeroplanes will fly at ten times the speed of sound (10 mach, 10 M); a speed of 7580 miles per hour within the next 30 years.

The table gives some speeds for you to look at. The blue whale swims at the same speed as a dragonfly flies!

What?	Speed in miles per hour
Aeroplane (fastest)	2274
Car (thrust)	766 (faster than speed of sound)
Cyclist (fastest)	132
Peregrine falcon (fastest animal and bird)	100–120
Cheetah (fastest land animal)	70
Dinosaur (Ornithomimid)	43
Blue whale (fastest marine animal)	30
Dragonfly (fastest insect)	30
Human (fastest)	23
100 year old man (fastest)	7
Sloth (slowest mammal)	0.07
Snail	0.03

Speed

To measure how fast something is moving we need to know:

* the distance it travels (measured in km, cm, miles, etc.)
* the time it takes (measured in seconds (s), minutes or hours).

$$\text{speed} = \frac{\text{distance}}{\text{time}}$$

The units of speed are km per hour (km/hour, km hr^{-1}), or miles per hour (miles/hour or miles hour^{-1}).

The equation for <u>speed</u> can be written in two other ways:

$$\text{distance} = \text{speed} \times \text{time}$$ and $$\text{time} = \frac{\text{distance}}{\text{time}}$$

23

Average speed

$$\text{Average speed} = \frac{\text{distance}}{\text{time}}$$

A car travels at an average speed of 30 miles per hour for 4 hours. How many miles does it travel?

distance $=$ speed $\times$ time
$30 \times 4 = 120$ miles

Graphs

The graphs below show distance against time and speed against time.

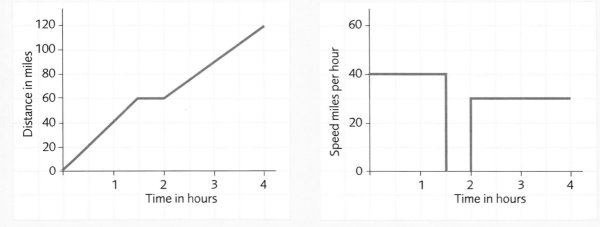

Distance against time   **Speed against time**

Notice that:

*   both graphs show a constant speed of 40 mph for the first hour and a half
*   on the distance/time graph, the steeper the line the greater the speed
*   on the speed/time graph, when the car is not moving the speed is zero.

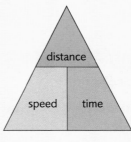
KEY FACTS

◁ speed $= \dfrac{\text{distance}}{\text{time}}$

- -

⊻ **The three equations relating speed, distance and time are:**

$$v = \frac{s}{t} \quad s = v \times t \quad \text{and} \quad t = \frac{s}{v}$$

(v = velocity (speed), s = distance, t = time)

- -

⊻ **Average speed is the total distance travelled divided by the time taken.**

- -

Quick, quick, slow

It was 6 May 1954. The time was announced. 'Three...' The rest was drowned out by the cheers. Roger Bannister had just become the first person to run a mile in under 4 minutes. His time was 3 minutes 59.4 seconds. For years, the 4-minute mile was considered impossible and dangerous to the health of any athlete who attempted it.

In 1999, the world record for the mile was 3 minutes 43.13 seconds. When Bannister ran his sub-four minute mile, timings were done to one-tenth of a second. Nowadays, timings for all World record attempts must be measured to one-hundredth of a second using fully automatic timing involving photography. In athletics, the mile and the marathon are the only non-metric world records that are still officially recognised.

Reaction time

The time that it takes you to react to a particular situation is called your reaction time. Your reaction time depends on many factors including:

- fatigue
- age
- eyesight
- alcohol consumption
- gender
- intelligence.

Reaction times are very important to drivers of cars. The slower their reaction times, the more likely they are to have an accident. In sports such as cricket, football, rugby, hockey and netball, reaction times can make the difference between winning and losing. The reaction times of police officers and fire-fighters are very important.

How do forces affect speed?

Forces can either speed up or slow down objects. A moving object usually has two forces slowing it down: friction and air resistance.

- In motor racing, cars are often driven close to the car in front. We say that they are in the 'slipstream' of the car in front; slipstreaming helps to save energy and fuel.
- In Space, a small thrust from a rocket increases the speed of a spacecraft.
- We use brakes on cars and lorries to slow them down.

When a state of constant speed is reached, the forward forces equal the forces in the opposite direction. (This is also true when an object is stationary; the forces acting in different directions balance one another.)

The diagram shows forces acting on a car. The arrows show the size and direction of the forces.

If stationary: moves forwards   remains stationary   goes backwards
If moving: accelerates   moves at a constant speed   slows down

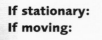

Other effects of forces

- **Changing direction**. Forces can make objects change direction. When you play tennis, you use force to make the ball change direction when you hit it back over the net. When walking down a busy pavement, you can avoid people by side-stepping; you put more force on one leg than on the other.
- **Turning**. When you use a spanner to undo a nut, you use a force to turn the nut. When ice skaters spin on ice, they are using a turning force to make them spin. And you use a turning force when you pull a tab of a drinks can.  
- **Changing shape**. In a gym, people change the shape of the apparatus they use. They might stretch or compress springs; they might bend or twist apparatus. If you've seen a car that's been in an accident, you will have seen the change in shape of the car caused by various forces exerted on it during the accident.

Size matters

The larger the object the more difficult it is to move.

- Imagine taking an elephant for a walk on a lead. It would be much easier to restrain a dog than an elephant.
- Small wheels are easier to turn than large wheels. Look at your bicycle and compare it with the old penny-farthing bicycles that were very difficult to ride.

KEY FACTS

- ◄ Unbalanced forces cause either a change of speed and/or a change of direction.
- ► If forces are balanced there is no change in movement.
- ◄ Large objects need more force to move them than do smaller objects.

EXAMINER'S TOP TIPS

You must give the units of speed, so make sure you have read the units for distance and time carefully. Distance will usually be measured in metres (m) and speed in seconds (s). The units of speed will be m/s or ms^{-1}.

3, 2, 1 jump!

When a skydiver jumps from an aeroplane, he will be travelling forward at the same speed as the aeroplane, which is about 110 mph at a height of about 3658 m (12 000 ft).

During the next 10 seconds he starts to fall and accelerates to a speed of about 130 mph.

The skydiver then reaches a constant speed of 124 mph.

After 70 seconds, at about 610 m (2000 ft) above the ground, the square parachute is opened. There is a huge 'snap-up' before the skydiver starts to descend.

The total time of the jump is about 100 seconds, plus the time it takes to land.

Skydiving explained

- When a skydiver jumps out of the plane he has the same forward speed as the plane. If several people jump, one after another, they will fall in a straight line.
- Two forces then start to act on the skydiver:
  - the downward force of gravity, and
  - the upward force of air.
- Initially a skydiver moves slowly, but, since the force of gravity is greater than air resistance, the skydiver speeds up. The skydiver starts accelerating towards the ground.
- Air resistance increases as speed increases; eventually the air resistance equals the force of gravity and the skydiver reaches a constant speed of 124 mph
- When the parachute is opened, there is a large increase in the air resistance causing the skydiver to be 'snapped' upwards.
- When the skydiver lands, his weight acting downwards is exactly balanced by an equal upward force from the ground.

There are other factors to consider:

- weight: the heavier the skydiver, the faster he will fall
- body position: the more spread out the bodily position of the skydiver is, the slower he will fall. The skydivers shown in the photograph above alter their body positions and hence their speed, so that they can catch up with one another. In a 'stand up' position, speeds of 180 mph can be reached. (The record sky speed fall is 321 mph.)

Height/time graph

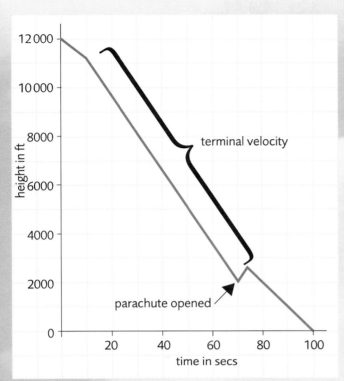

The graph shows height against time for a skydiver. Reading the graph you can see that he dived out of the plane at 12 000 ft. He fell slowly at first and then reach his terminal velocity. At 2000 ft he deployed his parachute and ascended a few hundred feet, before drifting to the ground.

His descent with the parachute was slower than when he was free falling.

After 90 seconds he used a special technique to slow him down for landing.

Air resistance

Gas is made up of small particles in a constant state of motion. When these particles hit a surface they cause <u>pressure</u>. It is the collision of these particles with the parachute that causes air resistance.

When a Space capsule returns and enters the Earth's atmosphere, the friction between air and the capsule causes the capsule to heat up. The temperature reached is about 1500 °C. (The capsule is fitted with special heat-resistant tiles.)

Reducing air resistance

Much research has been done on how to reduce air resistance.

- Cars have been designed to make them streamlined and lorries have wind deflectors, reducing air resistance and thus fuel consumption, making them more economic to run.
- Clothing worn by athletes and swimmers has been designed to reduce air resistance.
- Tall buildings are designed so that wind passes around them.

KEY FACTS

◄ **Gravity pulls all objects to the centre of the Earth.**

◄ **Terminal velocity is reached when the downward force (weight) is equal to the upward force (air resistance).**

EXAMINER'S TOP TIPS

If you are asked to draw arrows to show forces, air resistance and friction always point towards the object and gravity points vertically downwards.

The pressure is on

- If a piece of very thin wire is placed around a block of ice and weights are hung on the ends of the wire it passes through the ice block but the ice is not cut in half. This is because the ice melts under the pressure of the wire and then re-freezes. The process is called <u>regelation</u>, which means 'to freeze again'.
- Regelation occurs only at temperatures at, or just below, 0°C. This is why you can make really good snowballs at temperatures near 0°C (the snow melts due to the pressure of your hands compressing it into a ball, and then re-freezes, holding the snowball together).
- Regelation is one of the factors that causes glaciers to move. The pressure of the glacier on the base of the glacier causes it to melt. This provides a smooth surface (reduced friction) on which the glacier moves.

What is pressure?

Regelation suggests that pressure depends on:

- the mass of an object
- the area on which the mass is acting.

$$\text{Pressure} = \frac{\text{force}}{\text{area}} \qquad \textbf{Pressure is the force acting on each } m^2 \text{ or } cm^2, \textbf{ of area.}$$

- Force is measured in newtons, so the units of force are N per m^2 (N/m^2 or Nm^{-2}).
- $1\,N/m^2$ is also known as 1 Pascal (Pa).
- If the area is small it is measured in cm^2 and the units will be N per cm^2 (N/cm^2 or Ncm^{-2}).

Would you rather have your foot stepped on by a:

(i) 50 kg woman wearing stiletto-heeled shoes with a heel area of 1 cm^2, or
(ii) 4500 kg elephant with a foot area of 1500 cm^2?

For woman

Pressure = $\frac{500}{1}$ = 500 N/m^2

For elephant

Pressure = $\frac{4500}{1500}$ = 30 N/m^2

Note: the mass has to be converted into a force (weight). It is better to be stepped on by an elephant than by a lady wearing stiletto heels!

Bed of nails

- Assume the man in the picture weighs 540 newtons and that each nail has an area of 0.01 cm^2.
- If there was one nail on the plank then the pressure on the man would be 54 000 N/cm^2, and the nail would easily pass through him.
- The plank usually has about 2000 nails, giving a total area of nails of 20 cm^2. The pressure is:

$$\frac{540}{20} = 27\,N/cm^2$$

This is why it is possible to lie on a bed of nails.
It is essential that all the nails are at the same height!

Pneumatics

'Pneumatic' means that something is inflated or operated by a gas. *Pneuma* is the Latin word for 'air'. The particles in gases are so far apart that they can be compressed. Examples of pneumatics are:

*   pneumatic drills: these convert the energy of compressed gas to mechanical energy
*   bicycle tyres and car tyres: these are filled with air under pressure
*   spray aerosols and air fresheners: these have a liquid sealed with a gas under pressure in a can; when the pressure is released, the liquid is forced out as a fine spray, called an aerosol. (Gases expand when heated. Any container holding gas under pressure will explode if it is put on a fire.)

Hydraulics

The particles in a liquid are close together and therefore liquids cannot be compressed. Hydraulic lifts and braking system on cars use this property.

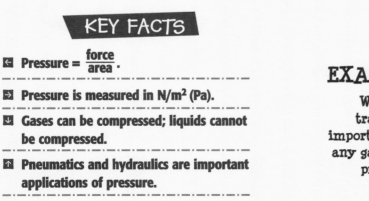

What force, X, must be applied to stop the plunger in the left-hand syringe from moving?

Pressure in right-hand syringe:

$$\frac{8}{2} = 4\,\text{N/cm}^2$$

This pressure is transferred to the left-hand syringe:

$$4 = \frac{X}{10} \quad \text{therefore } X = 40\,\text{N}$$

By applying a small force (8 N) you are able to lift, or move, a bigger force (40 N). But, the small force has to move further in order to lift the larger force a small distance. In the above example, when the small plunger moves 5 cm, the large plunger moves 1 cm.

When a force is applied by the foot to the brake pedal of a car, the brakes on the wheels only have to move a small amount before they start to slow the car down.

KEY FACTS

◄ **Pressure = $\frac{\text{force}}{\text{area}}$** .

→ **Pressure is measured in N/m² (Pa).**

↓ **Gases can be compressed; liquids cannot be compressed.**

↑ **Pneumatics and hydraulics are important applications of pressure.**

EXAMINER'S TOP TIPS

When a liquid is used for transferring pressure, it is important that it does not contain any gas. Gases are compressed by pressure; liquids are not.

Move it!

The instructions for erecting the stones at Stonehenge in about 2500 BC could have been along the following lines.

1   Dig a hole about 3 ft deep.

2   Use rollers to slide the stone to the edge of the hole.

3   Lever the stone up and put rocks underneath it to keep it off the ground.

4   Repeat until the stone is at an angle of 45°.

5   Now go to the other side and use a rope to pull the stone upright into the hole.

6   Fill the hole with small stones and earth until it is firmly in place.

7   Repeat 29 times to make a circle 90 ft in diameter.

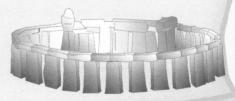

(Note: There would have been more complex instructions using platforms and levers to put the cross pieces in position.)

Levers

We use <u>levers</u> every day of our lives, e.g. opening a door, cutting with a pair of scissors or lifting something up.

A lever is a simple machine that turns about a fixed point called the pivot (fulcrum). A lever does two important things. It changes the:

* position at which the force acts
* effect of the force (makes it bigger or smaller).

Levers can be used to produce either a large force or a large movement.

Everyday uses of levers

In the following examples, *E* is the effort (force needed to move an object) applied at one point of the lever; *L* is the load (the force to be moved) at another point of the lever; and *P* is the pivot.

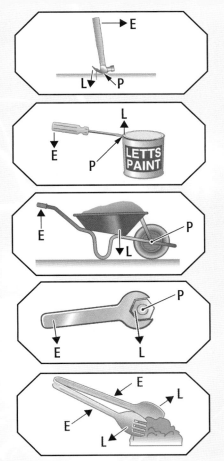

- A claw hammer is used to pull out nails. A large force is required. The pivot is between the load and the effort. The effort moves a large distance and the load moves a short distance.

- Opening a tin of paint with a screwdriver. A large force is required. It is easier to remove the lid with a screwdriver than with a coin.

- In a wheelbarrow the pivot is nearer the load. It is designed so that a small effort is needed to lift a large load. Nutcrackers and bottle openers have a similar design. When you close a door (load), it is easier if you push (effort) the handle, than if you push it near the hinges (pivot).

- In a spanner the pivot is near the load. Nuts are usually very tightly screwed on. The design of the spanner gives you the best possible opportunity to undo the nut. The longer the spanner, the easier it is to unscrew the nut.

- In sugar tongs the effort is between the load and the pivot. This type of lever produces a large movement from a small movement. In games that involve hitting a ball, your body is the pivot, your arm and hand the effort and the ball the load at the end of the lever.

Muscles are levers

Your arms bend and straighten when you use your biceps and triceps muscles. The elbow acts as the pivot. When your biceps muscle contracts, your arm bends. When your triceps muscle contracts, your arm straightens. The muscles work together but in opposite directions. Because they work in opposite directions they are called <u>antagonistic</u> <u>muscles</u>.

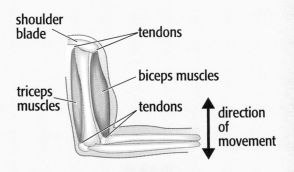

KEY FACTS

- ◁ A lever is a simple machine that turns about a fixed point called the pivot.

- ▷ Levers can be used to produce a larger force or a larger movement.

- ▽ Antagonistic muscles are muscles that work in opposite directions.

EXAMINER'S TOP TIPS

To understand how a lever works, work out the direction of the load and effort forces and where the pivot is.

Just a moment...

Tightrope Walker Crosses Niagara Falls

A tightrope walker called Charles Blondin crossed Niagara Falls on a tightrope at night, backwards, blindfolded on stilts, with his manager on his back (no one else would volunteer). He even sat on a chair drinking a glass of champagne!

Moments

A force may cause an object to turn about a pivot. The 'turning effect' of a force is called its <u>moment</u>.

The moment of a force depends upon two factors:

*   the size of the force
*   the perpendicular distance of the force from the point.

> **Moment = force x perpendicular distance of the force from the point**

The units of force are Nm.
Note: It must be the *perpendicular distance* of the force from the point.

The principle of moments

The principle states that: 'When a system is balanced the sum of the clockwise moments about a pivot is equal to the sum of the anticlockwise moments about the same pivot.'

*   In the diagram below, positions can be moved until the children are balanced.

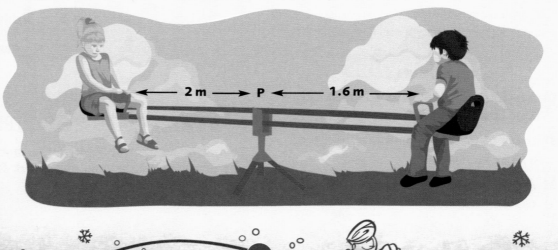

- The girl's clockwise moment is:

  > **200 (her weight) × 2 (distance from P) = 400 Nm**

- The boy's anticlockwise moment is:

  > **250 (his weight) × 1.6 (distance from P) = 400 Nm**

- Because:

  > **clockwise moments = anticlockwise moments**

  the see-saw is balanced.

- If the boy moved and sat 1.0 m from the pivot, his moment would be 250 × 1 = 250 Nm. The girl would have to move to a position 1.25 m from the pivot (200 × 1.25 = 250 Nm) to make the see-saw balance.

Everyday use of moments

The building crane (tower crane) is used for constructing tall buildings. The long horizontal part of the crane is called the jib. This is the part that carries the load. The short horizontal part is called the machinery arm. It contains the large concrete counter weights, and also the operator's cab, motors and electronics.

The arms of the crane are made to balance by moving the load on the long arm and the load on the short arm until the moments are equal.

(Large bolts embedded in a very large lump of concrete also bolt the crane to the ground.)

EXAMINER'S TOP TIPS

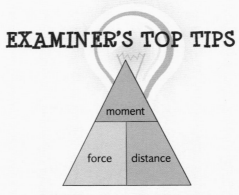

moment

force | distance

Use this triangle to work out the relationships between the three functions.

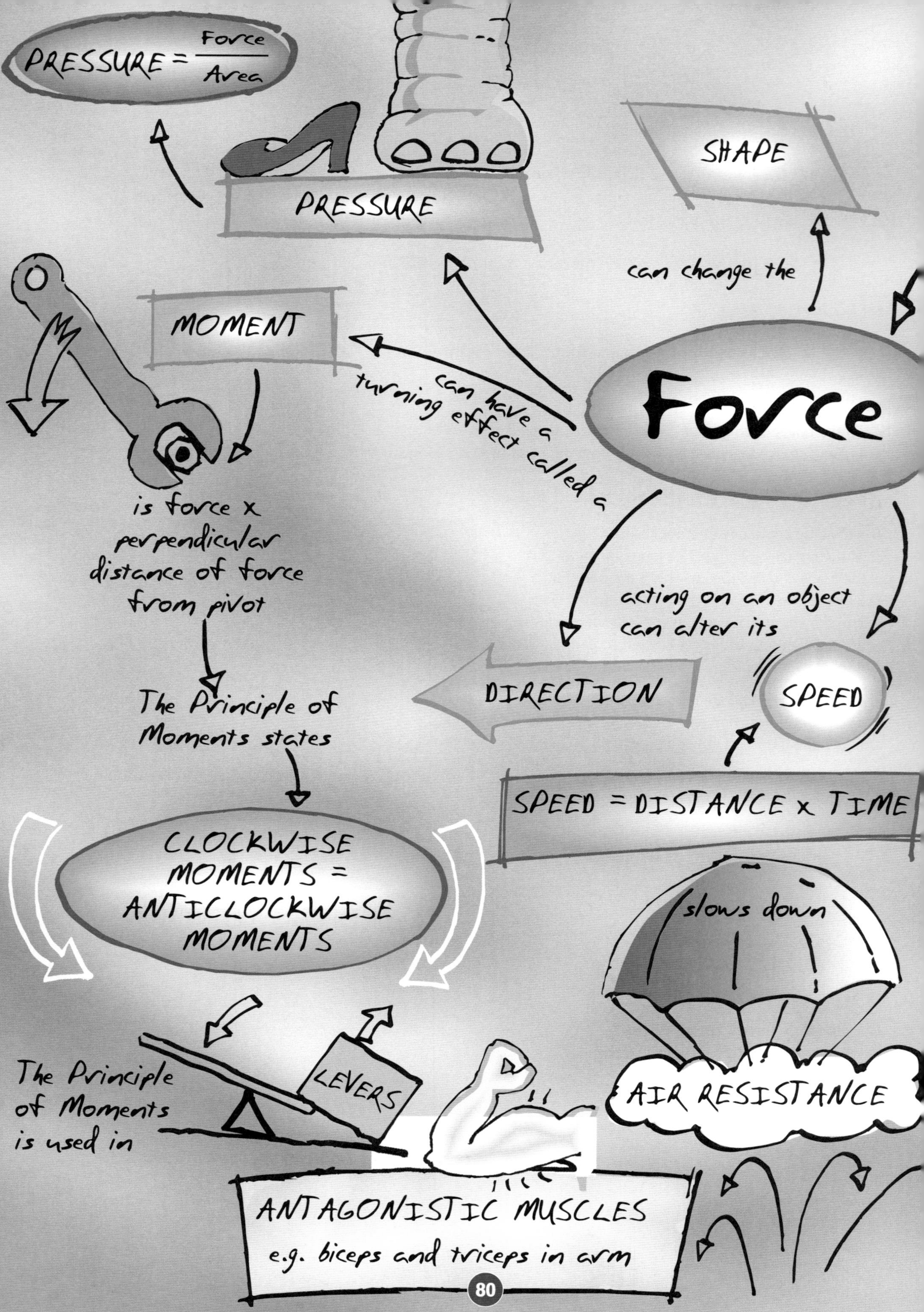

$$\text{PRESSURE} = \frac{\text{Force}}{\text{Area}}$$

PRESSURE

SHAPE

can change the

MOMENT

can have a turning effect called a

Force

is force x perpendicular distance of force from pivot

acting on an object can alter its

The Principle of Moments states

DIRECTION

SPEED

SPEED = DISTANCE x TIME

CLOCKWISE MOMENTS = ANTICLOCKWISE MOMENTS

slows down

The Principle of Moments is used in

LEVERS

AIR RESISTANCE

ANTAGONISTIC MUSCLES
e.g. biceps and triceps in arm

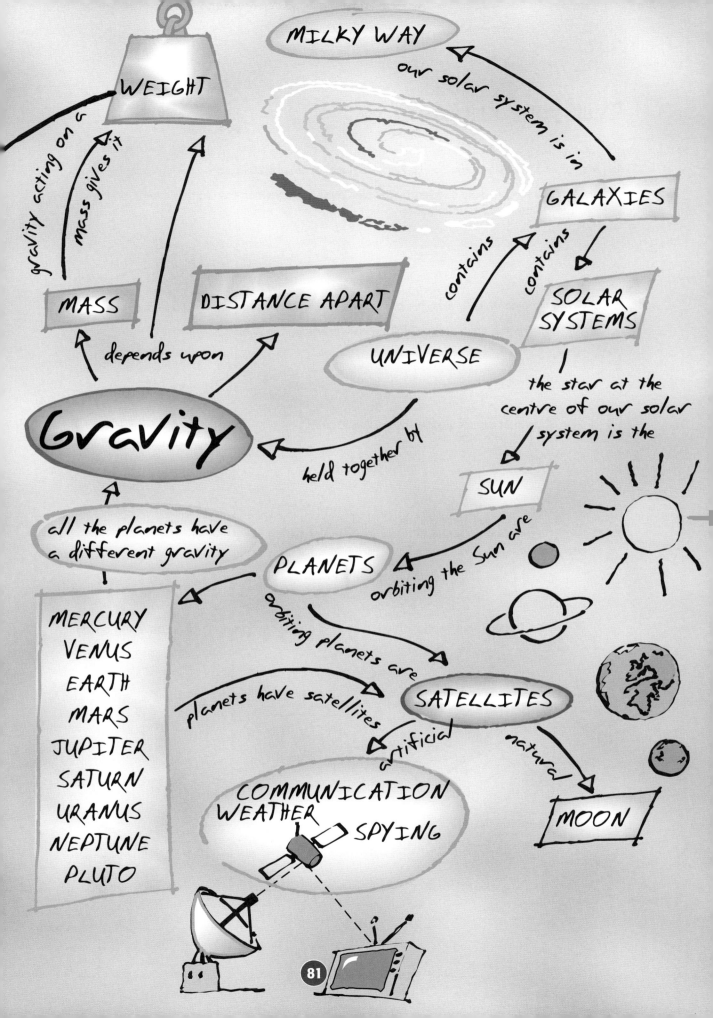

WEIGHT

gravity acting on a

mass gives it

MILKY WAY

our solar system is in

GALAXIES

contains

contains

SOLAR SYSTEMS

MASS

DISTANCE APART

UNIVERSE

depends upon

Gravity

held together by

the star at the centre of our solar system is the

SUN

all the planets have a different gravity

PLANETS

orbiting the Sun are

MERCURY
VENUS
EARTH
MARS
JUPITER
SATURN
URANUS
NEPTUNE
PLUTO

orbiting planets are

planets have satellites

SATELLITES

artificial

natural

COMMUNICATION
WEATHER
SPYING

MOON

Test your knowledge 4

1 A skier and her skis weigh 750 N. Her skis have an area of 2500 cm^2.

a) What is the pressure exerted by the skis on the snow when the woman stands on the snow? Include the units in your answer.

b) When she carries her skis, her pressure is five times as large as when she was wearing skis.

(i) What is the pressure the woman now exerts on the snow?

(ii) Show that the area of her boots is 500 cm^2.

c) If the woman skis downhill at a steady speed of 15 m/s, how long would it take her, in minutes, to complete a 1800 m course?

d) (i) Label the diagram to show the forces A, B and C acting on this skier travelling downhill.

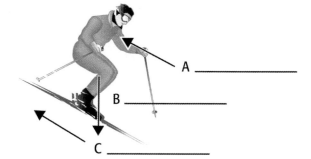

A _____

B _____

C _____

(ii) Which force A, B or C will be greatest? How do you know this?

....

....

....

(14 marks)

2 a) (i) What is a geostationary satellite?

....

....

....

   (ii) Give one use of a geostationary satellite.

....

b) Words used to describe material in Space are:

galaxy   part of the Universe   planet   satellite   star   Solar System,

   (i) The Moon is a natural satellite of the Earth. What does this statement mean?

....

....

....

   (ii) Mars is a planet. It is part of the Solar System and part of the Universe. This is shown in the table below by using ticks (✓).

   Complete the table below for (i) the Earth; (ii) the Sun; and (iii) the Milky Way.

	Mars	Earth	Sun	Milky Way
a galaxy				
part of the Universe	✓			
planet	✓			
star				
part of the Solar System	✓			

(8 marks)

(Total 22 marks)

Practice paper

Allow 90 minutes to complete the following questions.

1   A footballer injured his knee. The diagram shows the damaged joint.

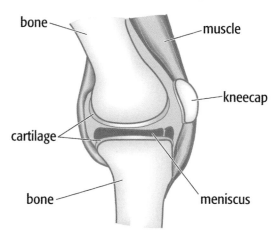

The following types of joints can be found in the human skeleton.

ball and socket   fixed   gliding   hinge   pivot

a)   (i)   Which type of joint is found in your knee?

....

(ii)   Where else in the skeleton is this type of joint found?

....

(iii)   Describe the movement made by this type of joint.

....

b)   What word is the missing in the following sentence?

.... join bones together and limit the movement in joints.

c)   Between the bones there is a cartilage-type material called the meniscus.

(i)   Why is the meniscus important during movement?

....

(ii)   Look at the diagram then suggest why the footballer has a severe pain in his knee when he tries to
walk or run.

....

d)   The body has two identical saddle joints. They can rock back and forth and from side to side. Suggest
where in your body you might find these joints.

....

(9 marks)

2   Circle the word in the brackets that best completes each sentence.

a) A flower produces fruit and seeds only after (photosynthesis / pollination / respiration / transpiration).

b) A male does NOT have (testes / hormones / a urethra / ovaries) in his body.

c) Between the uterus and the vagina is the (urethra / placenta / zygote / cervix).

d) In the uterus, the embryo is connected to the placenta by the (fetus / umbilical cord / zygote / oviduct).

e) Menstruation occurs (after / before / just before / during) ovulation.

f) The male reproductive system of a plant is the (petal / sepal / stamen / stem).

(6 marks)

3   There are two forms of cell division, *meiosis* and *mitosis*. The table contains statements about cell division.

a) For each statement place a tick (✓) in the appropriate column of the table.

Statement	Mitosis only	Meiosis only
asexual reproduction		
replaces worn out body cells		
production of gametes		

b) Suggest why mature red blood cells do NOT reproduce by mitosis.

....

....

....

....

(4 marks)

4 Part of the reactivity series for metals is shown below.

sodium (most reactive)
calcium
magnesium
aluminium
(carbon)
zinc
iron
lead
(hydrogen)
copper (least reactive)

a) Why have carbon and hydrogen been put in brackets?

....

b) Which metal occurs naturally?

....

c) Why is sodium kept under oil?

....

....

d)

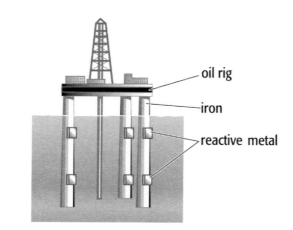

oil rig

iron

reactive metal

The diagram shows an oil rig which has large pieces of a reactive metal attached to the iron supports to stop them rusting. The blocks of metal corrode instead of the iron.

(i) What is rusting?

....

(ii) Name a suitable metal that could be attached to the pipes to stop them from rusting.

....

(iii) Name a metal that could not be used to stop the iron from rusting. Give a reason for your answer.

Metal: ....

Reason: ....

e) Suggest why jam is made in copper pans and not in aluminium pans.

....

....

(11 marks)

5 When magnesium is burned in air, the reaction is exothermic.

a) (i) What is meant by *exothermic*?

....

(ii) What chemical word is the opposite of exothermic?

....

b) Write (i) the word equation and (ii) the symbol equation for magnesium burning in air.

(i) word equation:

....

(ii) symbol equation:

....

c) When magnesium burns in carbon dioxide, a black solid and a white solid are formed. Name these two compounds.

(i) black solid: ....

(ii) white solid: ....

d) Magnesium reacts with steam to form hydrogen and magnesium oxide.

(i) Why can firefighters NOT use water hoses to put out the fire?

....

....

(ii) Suggest the method firefighters might use to put out a magnesium fire.
     Give a reason for your answer.

Method to put out fire: ....

Reason: ....

....

e) A firefighter has to give a person the kiss of life. (Mouth-to-mouth resuscitation until normal breathing is resumed by the patient.) What gas must expired air contain in order for this form of resuscitation to be successful?

....

(14 marks)

6   In the following two circuits, the bulbs B1, B2 and B3 used are identical; the switches S1, S2 and S3 used are identical; and the batteries used are identical.

For each circuit circle 'T' for 'True' or 'F' for 'false' at the end of each statement to show whether it is true or false.

a)   Circuit 1:

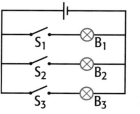

   (i)   When S2 and S3 are on, B1 will be lit.   T / F
   (ii) If B1 bulb 'blows' and S1 and S3 are on, B3 will be lit.   T / F
   (iii) When S1 is on, B1 is brighter than when S1, S2 and S3 are on.   T / F

b)   Circuit 2:

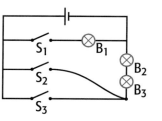

   (i)   When S2 and S3 are on, B1 will be lit.   T / F
   (ii) When S2 is on, B2 and B3 will be lit.   T / F
   (iii) When S3 is on, B2 and B3 will be lit.   T / F
   (iv) When S1, S2 and S3 are all on, B1, B2 and B3 will have the same brightness.   T / F
   (v)   If the voltage from the cell was increased, B1 would be brighter and B2 and B3
          would be less bright.   T / F

c)   Draw a circuit such that when either S1, S2 or S3 is on, B1, B2 and B3 are all on.

(11 marks)

7   In pole vaulting, kinetic energy is converted into potential energy.

a)   What is (i) kinetic energy (ii) potential energy?

   (i)   kinetic energy: ....

   (ii) potential energy: ....

          ....

The diagram shows a pole vaulter, Dale, at the start of his run-up.

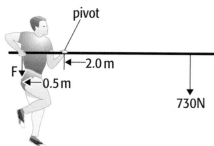

pivot

F

←2.0 m

←0.5 m

730N

b) (i) What is the Dale's potential energy at the start of his run-up?

....

(ii) The weight of the pole is 730 N. Assume the left hand is the pivot.

The right hand is 0.5 m from the left hand. The weight of the pole acts at a distance of 2.0 m from the left hand.

What force must Dale apply with his right hand to keep the pole level? Show all your working.

c) Dale covers his run up of 45 m in 5 seconds.

(i) Show that Dale's average speed is 9 m/s. You must write down the formula that you used to make your calculation.

(ii) Dale's kinetic energy at take off is 2880 Joules. What is his potential energy at the top of his jump? State how you reached your conclusion.

....

....

d) The height Dale jumps can be calculated using the formula:

$$h = \frac{v^2}{2g}$$ (h is height, and g is the force of gravity = 10 m s^{-2})

What height can Dale jump?

e) Potential energy, in Joules, is equal to weight x height. If Dale, who has a mass of 710 N, lands on a soft mat 2 m from the ground, what is his kinetic energy when he lands?

(15 marks)

(Total 70 marks)

Glossary

Acid rain Rain containing harmful amounts of nitric acid and sulphuric acid formed by oxides of nitrogen and sulphur which are released when fossil fuels are burned.

Acidic oxide An oxide of a non-metal.

Addiction State in which a person has a physical and mental need.

Alkali A base that is soluble in water.

Allele An alternative form of a gene.

Alveoli Tiny air spaces in the lung where oxygen is exchanged for carbon dioxide.

Ammeter An instrument that measures the size of an electric current.

Antagonistic muscles Muscles that work in opposite directions.

Asexual reproduction Reproduction in which a single individual copies its generic material.

Atmosphere The mass of air that surrounds the Earth.

Ball and socket joint Produces circular movement, e.g. hip and shoulder.

Base (in genetics) There are four, represented by the letters A, T, G, C. Their sequence in DNA determines cell information.

Base (in metals) An oxide or hydroxide of a metal.

Basic oxide An oxide that reacts with water to form a base.

Biomass All the organic matter produced by photosynthesis that exists on the Earth's surface.

Budding A method of cloning.

Carbon dioxide An atmospheric gas made up of one carbon and two oxygen atoms.

Catalyst Speeds up a reaction without changing itself.

Chemical energy The energy stored in a substance.

Chemical reaction A reaction in which a new substance is formed and there is an energy change.

Chemical properties Behaviour of a substance in chemical reactions.

Chlorofluorocarbons CFCs Organic compounds composed of chlorine, fluorine and carbon atoms.

Chlorophyll The green pigment in plant cells that captures energy from sunlight necessary for photosynthesis.

Chloroplast The organelle in a plant cell that contains chlorophyll and is the site of photosynthesis.

Chromosome Thread-like strand in the nucleus that controls cell activity. It carries genetic material to pass traits to offspring.

Cloning The process of making genetically identical copies.

Common salt Sodium chloride (NaCl).

Complete protein A readily digestible protein.

Consumer An organism that eats other living things.

Cuticle The waxy coating on the outer surface of leaves.

Displacement reaction A reaction in which an element sets free an element from a compound.

DNA (deoxyribonucleic acid) A double-stranded helix that carries the genetic information of a cell.

Dominant allele The allele that determines the phenotype.

Drug Any substance that changes the way your body or mind works.

Electrolyte Made up of ions that are free to move when melted or in solution. Can be acids, alkalis, bases or salts.

Endothermic Takes in heat energy.

Energy The ability to do work.

Epidermis The outer layer, beneath the cuticle, which helps to protect the leaf.

Etiolated Plant that develops without chlorophyll by being deprived of light.

Eutrophication When fertilisers in water stimulate the growth of plants.

Exothermic Gives out heat energy.

Fertilisation When a male gamete (sperm) fuses with a female gamete (ovum).

Fertilisers Substance added to the soil to increase its productivity.

Food chain Sequence of organisms through which food energy passes.

Forcemeter Instrument measuring force (units are a Newton).

Fossil fuel A fuel, e.g. coal, oil and natural gas, produced by the decomposition of plants and animals millions of years ago.

Fuel Substance that burns easily to form heat and light.

Galaxy Independent system of billions of stars bound together by gravity.

Gamete A sex cell having a single set of unpaired chromosomes. It unites with another gamete to form a zygote.

Gene Functional and physical unit of heredity that determines the trait.

Gene therapy Process to replace a damaged or changed gene with a healthy gene.

Genetic code Information existing in the sequence of the four bases in DNA.

Genome (human) All the genetic material in a human cell.

Genotype Gene combination that determines the phenotype.

Geostationary Satellite that moves in an orbit so that it remains above the same point on the Earth's surface.

Grafting Method of cloning.

Gravity Force of attraction between all masses in the Universe, especially the attraction of the Earth's mass for bodies near its surface.

Greenhouse effect The effect of carbon dioxide and methane in keeping the Earth's surface warmer than it would be otherwise.

Group (in Periodic Table) Vertical group of elements showing similar properties, e.g. Group I, metals.

Herbicide Chemicals used to kill unwanted plants, e.g. weeds.

Herbivore An organism that eats plants only.

Hinge joint Produces movement in single plane, e.g. knee and elbow.

Identical twins Develop from a single zygote. The twins have identical DNA, i.e. the same genotype but different phenotype.

Incomplete protein A protein lacking some parts.

Inorganic fertiliser Enhances plant growth. Made artificially. Contains high concentrations of minerals.

Insecticide Chemicals used to kill insect pests, e.g. mosquitoes.

Joint Place where two or more bones meet.

Lever Simple machine that turns about a fixed point.

Malleable Metals can be moulded.

Meiosis Cell division process that eggs and sperm go through that halves the number of chromosomes.

Methane A gas produced by animal waste.

Minerals Nutrients needed by plants to thrive.

Mitosis Process by which a cell nucleus divides into two identical nuclei.

Moment Turning effect of a force. It is force x perpendicular distance of force from the pivot.

Moon A natural satellite that circles a planet.

Mutation A fault that occurs in a gene. Can cause abnormal body processes.

Neutralised An acid added to an alkali in the correct proportions produces a neutral solution of pH 7.

Newton Force which, if applied for one second, will cause a mass of 1 kilogram starting from rest, to reach a speed of 1 m/s.

Non-identical twins Two different eggs are fertilised and develop in the uterus at the same time.

Nuclear fission The splitting of a large nucleus into smaller nuclei with the release of energy.

Nutrients Essential elements needed for plants to thrive, e.g. nitrogen.

Omnivore Organism that eats plants and animals.

Orbit Path taken by a satellite or planet.

Organic fertiliser Enhances plant growth. Made by natural means, e.g. manure.

Organic food Produced without the use of chemicals.

Ozone layer Layer of ozone around the World that acts as a filter against ultraviolet radiation.

Palisade cell In a leaf, contain chloroplasts for photosynthesis.

Parallel circuit Components in an electric circuit are connected so that they can be operated independently.

Periodic Table Classification of the elements in a table to show trends.

Pesticide Chemicals used to kill pests.

pH Measure on a scale from 0 to 14 of the acidity or alkalinity of a solution, pH 7 is neutral.

Phenotype Trait that an organism shows.

Photosynthesis Process by which plants use energy from sunlight to convert water and carbon dioxide into carbohydrates and oxygen. Oxygen is produced by this process.

Physical properties Those properties of a substance other than its chemical interactions, e.g. its melting point.

Planet Celestial body moving round a star in an elliptical orbit.

Polymerise Joining together of small molecules (monomers) to form a very large molecule (polymer).

Predator Animal that hunts and kills other animals for its food.

Pressure Force per unit area.

Producer At the bottom of the food chain, e.g. grass.

Reactivity series The order of reactivity of metals.

Recessive allele Is only expressed if both alleles in a pair are recessive.

Regelation Ice melting under pressure and freezing again when pressure is released.

Respiration Process by which glucose is broken down into carbon dioxide and water.

Salt Compound formed when the hydrogen in an acid is replaced by a metal or 'ammonium'.

Satellite Celestial body orbiting a planet. Or a man-made structure launched into orbit in Space.

Selective breeding Selecting desirable traits and cross-breeding to obtain combined traits in some of the offspring.

Series circuit Components cannot be operated independently.

Sex chromosomes Determine the sex of offspring.

Simple cell The simplest type of battery. Consists of two terminals and an electrolyte.

Solar System The area of Space occupied by Earth, Sun and known planets.

Speed Distance travelled in unit time.

Spongy layer In a leaf, air-filled spaces for gas exchange.

Staple food A food that forms the basis of a diet, e.g. corn or rice.

State symbols (in chemical equations) Describes the state of a substance, e.g. gas (g), liquid (l), solid (s) or aqueous (aq).

Stoma (plural stomata) Small opening on the surface of a plant that is used for gas exchange.

Sun Star at the centre of our Solar System.

Thermit process Displacement reaction where aluminium displaces iron in iron oxide in a violent reaction hot enough to weld broken railway tracks.

Trait A distinguishing feature of your personal nature.

Transition metals Occupy space in the Periodic Table between Groups II and III. Share similar properties.

Variegated plants Leaves are of two or more colours.

Voltmeter Instrument that measures the voltage across an appliance.

X chromosome Longer than Y chromosome. Carried in both male and female gametes.

Y chromosome Shorter than X chromosome. Carried only in male gamete.

Zygote Cell formed by the union of an ovum and a sperm.

Answers

Test your knowledge 1

1 a) 64

b) 32

c) (i) Paul must be cc, he is NOT curly haired.

(ii) Emily must be Cc. Imogen has straight hair so must be cc. One c has to come from Emily.

(iii)

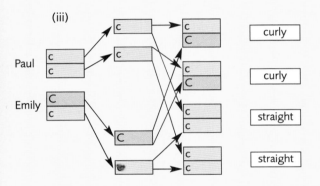

Two curly haired, two straight haired, so the chances are 50:50.

(iv) Every child that Imogen and her partner have will be curly haired.

2 a) Carbon monoxide is the only neutral gas, so it will not dissolve in sodium hydroxide.

b) carbon, hydrogen, nitrogen and sulphur (the oxygen could have come from the air).

c) nicotine

3

Percentage of substance in exhaled air	More/less/ same
carbon dioxide	more
nitrogen and noble gases	same
oxygen	less
water vapour	more

Test your knowledge 2

1 a) (i) magnesium and sulphuric acid

(ii) no more hydrogen given off/excess of magnesium left

b) (i) base
(ii) zinc nitrate

c) (i) carbon dioxide

(ii) no more gas given off

d) (i) a soluble base

(ii) SALT + WATER

2 a) oxygen

b) (i) carbon dioxide

(ii) water

c) carbon dioxide + water → glucose + oxygen

d) (i) sunlight

(ii) chlorophyll

3 a) add iodine solution – goes black if starch is present.

b) (i) C
(ii) Photosynthesis will only take place where there is chlorophyll (the green area) and sunlight.

c) So that no starch was formed in the leaf before the experiment started.

Test your knowledge 3

1 a) (i) copper

(ii) 3.1 °C

(iii) exothermic, there is a rise in temperature

b)

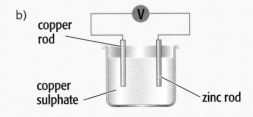

2 a) A thermal energy; B steam pushing piston; C kinetic energy

   b) (i) light energy; (ii) sound energy

   c) heat energy

   d) (i) sulphur dioxide; (ii) carbon monoxide

   e) Electric trams are more energy efficient.

3
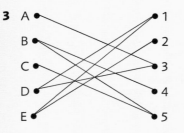

b) (i) A celestial body that orbits the Earth.

(ii)

	Mars	Earth	Sun	Milky Way
a galaxy				✓
part of the Universe	✓	✓	✓	✓
planet	✓	✓		
star			✓	
part of the Solar System	✓	✓	✓	

Test your knowledge 4

1 a) Pressure $= \dfrac{750}{2500} = 0.3$ N cm^{-2}

   b) (i) New pressure will be $0.3 \times 5 = 1.5$ Ncm^{-2}

   (ii) Area of boots $= \dfrac{750}{1.5} = 500$ cm^2

   c) time $= \dfrac{1800}{15} = 120$ seconds $= 2$ minutes

   d) (i) A air resistance; B gravity; C friction
   (ii) gravity – because he is moving down the hill

2 a) (i) A satellite that moves in an orbit so that it remains above the same point on the Earth's surface.

   (ii) communications

Practice paper answers

1 a) (i) hinge

(ii) elbow

(iii) bend backwards and forwards in same plane

b) ligaments

c) (i) acts as a soft sponge (spring)

(ii) a piece has been torn off the meniscus

d) thumbs

(9 marks)

2 a) pollination; b) ovaries; c) urethra;
d) umbilical cord; e) after; f) stamen

(6 marks)

3 a)

Statement	Mitosis only	Meiosis only
asexual reproduction	✓	
replaces worn out body cells	✓	
production of gametes		✓

b) they do not contain a nucleus

(4 marks)

4 a) they are non-metals

b) copper

c) because it reacts with oxygen and water vapour in the air

d) (i) the formation of reddish-brown iron oxides on iron by reaction with oxygen in the presence of water

(ii) magnesium, aluminium or zinc but not sodium or calcium

(iii) sodium or magnesium; they react with water

e) jam contains acids – it will remove the oxide layer from the aluminium pan and then react with the aluminium; copper is unreactive.

(11 marks)

5 a) (i) reaction that gives out heat energy

(ii) endothermic

b) (i) magnesium + oxygen → magnesium oxide

(ii) $2Mg + O_2 \rightarrow 2MgO$

c) (i) carbon; (ii) magnesium oxide

d) (i) water would turn to steam and react the magnesium

(ii) cover it with sand or special blanket to stop oxygen getting to the fire

e) must contain oxygen

(14 marks)

6 a) (i) F; (ii) T; (iii) F

b) (i) F ; (ii) T; (iii) T; (iv) F; (v) T

c)

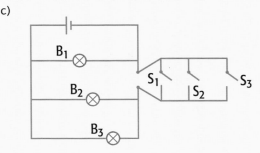

(11 marks)

7 a) (i) the energy an object has when it is moving

(ii) the energy and object has due to its position

b) (i) 0

(ii) clockwise moments = anticlockwise moments

$$730 \times 2 = \text{force} \times 0.5$$
$$\text{force} = 2920 \text{ newtons}$$

c) (i) speed = $\dfrac{\text{distance}}{\text{time}} = \dfrac{45}{5} = 9 \text{ ms}^{-1}$

(ii) 2880 Joules. All his kinetic energy will have been converted into potential energy.

d) $\dfrac{9 \times 9}{2 \times 10} = 4.05$ m

e) Potential energy = 710 x 2 = 1420 J, hence kinetic energy = 2880 – 1420 = 1460 J.

(15 marks)